L11

£2.50

MY GREAT BRITONS

Also by Emlyn Hughes
Crazy Horse

—MY—
GREAT BRITONS
EMLYN HUGHES

PARTRIDGE PRESS

LONDON · NEW YORK · TORONTO · SYDNEY · AUCKLAND

TRANSWORLD PUBLISHERS LTD
61–63 Uxbridge Road, London W5 5SA

TRANSWORLD PUBLISHERS (AUSTRALIA) PTY LTD
15–23 Helles Avenue, Moorebank, NSW 2170

TRANSWORLD PUBLISHERS (NZ) LTD
Cnr Moselle and Waipareira Aves,
Henderson, Auckland

Published 1988 by Partridge Press
a division of Transworld Publishers Ltd
Copyright © Emlyn Hughes 1988

British Library Cataloguing in Publication Data
Hughes, Emlyn
    My great britons.
    1. Great Britain. Sports. Biographies.
    Collections
    I. Title
    796'.092'2

ISBN 1–85225–023–2

Printed in West Germany by
Mohndruck Graphische Betriebe GmbH, Gütersloh
Typeset in 10/11.5 Palatino by
Photoprint, Torquay, Devon

*For Barb, Emma and Emlyn – with thanks
for being there when I get home*

Contents

Preface

The British love their sport. Tens of thousands of
fans will turn up in all weathers to watch the
great sporting events: the cup finals, the grand
prix races, the rugby internationals, the classic
race meetings and the Test matches. Millions will
sit up to all hours to watch televised sport
whether it is the Super Bowl final transmitted live
by satellite from across the world, or the late
finish of a snooker match coming from one of the
British venues such as the Crucible in Sheffield.
It's because of this fanatical following that the
leading sports stars of Britain are able to enjoy a
privileged position in our society.

I know that when I was playing with Liverpool
Football Club we were never allowed to forget
the importance of our wonderful fans. Not that it
would have been easy, with the Kop cheering
your every move, but the management always
took great pains to remind us of the debt we
owed. I don't believe a single Liverpool player
has ever been knowingly rude or discourteous to
a fan, and that's a record I'm proud to be
associated with.

Since I left full-time professional football I have
been able, in a small way, to put something back
into the world of sport. And at the same time I've
been able to look at sport from a slightly broader
perspective than when I was playing soccer
seven days a week. I've seen some of the great
triumphs and disasters, often at close hand, and
I've witnessed some of the sad and some of the

funny events that are all part and parcel of sporting competition. Most of all I've been able to meet the top sports stars, either through my work on television or at personal appearances and charity shows up and down the country. I've been fortunate to have stood on the same platform or shared the same microphone with some of the greatest names in British, and world, sport.

Being what I am, naturally inquisitive and not very shy(!), I have always taken the chance to chat to these men and women and to ask them about themselves, their lives in sport – and their lives out of it. Indeed, it has become such a habit of mine that it was suggested that I interview some of them more formally, those that I felt were especially interesting and had something to say, and, most importantly, those that had made a major contribution to sport in Britain.

What a challenge, and what a privilege. My list of Great Britons, as you can see, covers many sports and many different types of sports person-ality. The only common factor is that they have all put something into sport in Britain, something more than can be captured by the record books alone.

I've interviewed Nigel Mansell, the man who kept a nation awake at four-thirty in the morning to witness his dramatic challenge for the Formula One World Drivers' Championship. I've spoken to Sean Kerly, the man who became the figure-head for a born-again sport, and John Lowe, the man who dragged darts from the back rooms of pubs and took it to Tahiti, Tokyo and the top of the television ratings. I've met the man on whose large shoulders British boxing's popularity is built, Frank Bruno, and the woman who quietly and efficiently proved that a hobby can become a career and, in so doing, became one of our most popular world champions, Nora Perry. I've also included a couple of my very own sporting heroes: George Best, who showed the British public the meaning of the word "genius"; and Her Royal Highness The Princess Royal, who proved her worth in world competition despite all the pressures put upon her.

When I wrote my autobiography, *Crazy Horse*, I tried hard to steer clear of the predictable. That's why there are no long reports of matches we had won or honours I had achieved. . .maybe just descriptions of one or two of the goals I scored! In this book, too, I hope I have avoided stating the obvious. The British public, as I know only too well from being associated with *A Question of Sport*, knows its sports facts and figures. Therefore, instead of lists of cups and trophies, I've tried to find out more about the people I'm interviewing. I've tried to discover how they started out in sport, to whom they feel they owe their success and what it is that drives them on. I've asked about attitudes to authority – and the press – and have tried to find out what makes them laugh. . . and what makes them tear their hair out in frustration. At times I've also been able to compare my own experiences with those of the stars I'm interviewing.

The answers I've received to my questions have often been surprising, frequently very candid and sometimes quite outrageous. I think the stars have sometimes found it easier to talk to me than to, say, a member of the press. Whatever the reason for their frankness, the whole project has turned out to be a most interesting and informative experience for me. I'm pleased to be able to share it with you and hope you enjoy reading the book.

Emlyn Hughes OBE, March 1988

David Coleman

the voice of sport

David Coleman is an acknowledged master of the art of television presenting. He has covered everything from Come Dancing *to royal weddings. In his youth he was a top runner and won the Manchester Mile in 1949. In journalism he started out as a newspaper reporter, later becoming editor of a local Cheshire paper. In 1958, he helped to launch* Grandstand, *and later presented both* Sportsnight *and* Match of the Day. *He is not only a top sports commentator, concentrating on athletics, but also the popular chairman of one of BBC television's top quiz shows,* A Question of Sport.

*E*very week at *A Question of Sport* we have a warm-up comedian. I always feel sorry for him because his instructions are to warm up the audience, get them in the mood, but not to get them laughing too much. If things start to get moving and the audience are really loving every minute of his routine. . .he's got to quieten them down a bit. That must be a dreadful feeling for a professional comedian who spends his life trying to make 'em laugh, only be told to stop them from laughing.

Anyway, he never seems to grumble too much about it. The work's not that hard, really, as he tells the same jokes every week. The day he gets an audience coming in for the second time he's going to be in trouble.

Like all comedians he's in tune with his audience and he's also got one eye on the clock. His act, however, is not of a set length. He just goes on until the studio manager tells him there's one minute left. When he gets this signal he rounds off his act by introducing the next act. It goes something like this:

"Now don't forget, ladies and gentlemen, you're here to enjoy yourselves. Have fun and make the most of your day out. You're going to witness a recording of *A Question of Sport* which has become, as you'll all agree, a British institution. And, talking of British institutions, I'd like you to give a very big hand to the man I call the 'Guvnor', David Coleman."

David always flinches at this joke at his expense but takes it all in good heart. The warmth of the welcome he receives each week from our audience is testament to his popularity.

In truth, of course, David requires no introduction. He is the voice of British sport. He's not only one of the most knowledgeable people in his profession, he's also one of the most interesting – and, believe me, the two don't always go together. So it didn't take me long to decide that, before I set out on my search for Emlyn's Great Britons, I ought to come to David first. I wanted him to comment on my proposed selection. I knew he would be able to guide me to the special characteristics of the people I was going to see. Also David, being the master interviewer that he is, might be able to give me some hints for the job that lay ahead.

We decided to meet at the BBC studios in Manchester, a place where David is so much at home. I was due to see Mike Gatting the next day and so asked David about Gatts first.

"With the Pakistan row so fresh in people's minds," David began, "there's been a lot written and said about Mike. I've read that's he's an artisan and that he's a sergeant-major rather than an officer. These statements were made as veiled criticisms but I tell you, Em, there's nothing wrong with being an artisan or a sergeant-major.

"Nobody has worked harder than Mike at achieving the grade. His early England performances were very tricky for him. With only a small number of Test matches played each year, and the constant clamouring for new names in the team, you don't get many chances to establish yourself. It was clear to everybody that Mike could do it. When he went out for England, unfortunately, something always seemed to go wrong. So he came up the hard way and deserves his success."

That seemed like unreserved praise for the man, but I wondered if David thought he was not the best choice as England captain. It wasn't the kind of question I could put to Mike directly, so I thought I'd ask David.

"As we sit here he's still England captain. By the time people read this, who knows what the selectors will have done? All I can say is that I don't know if there's anybody better equipped to lead the England side at the present time. And look at the material he's had available. No other international Test side expects to do well when four or five of their top players have decided not to tour.

"If we're being perfectly honest about the situation, Em, I'm very glad he's got the job. His appointment proved a lot about cricket. Today, if you're good enough the background doesn't matter. It wasn't always like that of course."

Talking about Mike Gatting was a good way for me to introduce David to the reasons for my selection. My Great Britons are sports men and women who have been great for their sport and great for Britain. On both counts Mike Gatting scored; on both counts the other likely candidate, Ian Botham, failed to score.

Let's be frank about this. Ian wouldn't lose a moment's sleep because Emlyn Hughes had left him out of his selection of Great Britons. I can almost hear him saying: "So what!" But perhaps this very attitude is at the root of Ian's problem. Perhaps he should worry – particularly when people like David Coleman can find reasons to reproach him.

"He's temporarily lost his way but one can never take away from him the successes he's had in the game. In statistical terms Ian has done more than Mike; he's a more likely match winner and he's also going to pull in bigger crowds than Mike. Botham has already been England captain of course. My feeling is that he will get himself back together, not least because he likes winning matches and he won't like being left out of the team. Perhaps, then, he'll shape up a bit and we'll see the old Both in action again. As we've seen in recent weeks there are two sides to the man. As soon as he realises that he's only a public figure because of his cricket, then perhaps he'll get back to doing what he's best at."

With phrases like "getting back together" being used, it wasn't long before David and I started talking about George Best, another prominent name on my list. Now, Besty is a bit special for me, but what did David think? Was he the best ever?

"I don't think you can say who was the best because it's impossible to compare players from one age with those of another. That's the classic argument for any – who was the greatest. To my mind his name could be up there with the greats, Pele, Di Stefano, Maradona, except he didn't play for long enough."

David's comment brought us back to the kind of problem we'd been touching on when discussing Ian Botham.

"I don't think you can compare the two," David added. "The only similarity lies in a self-destructive streak. But Besty was a lovely man, would do anything for anybody and in that probably lay the seeds of his eventual downfall.

"I can remember doing a series of evenings with George where we'd be on stage talking about sport and answering questions. All the audience ever wanted to know was why George had a drink problem and what an alcoholic really was. They'd ask stupid questions about whether they, that is members of the audience, were drinking too much. George used to handle it really well. He sometimes told a story, not new but worth re-telling, about when he was courting Miss World.

"It appears that George was out on the town with this Miss World one night and wins about ten grand at gambling. They go back to their hotel and there's an Irish porter in the lobby. This porter pays Besty some compliments and, when George asks for some champagne, offers to bring it up to the room himself.

"So George and Miss World go up to the room and while she's sitting up in bed waiting for her drink, George decides to count the money he's just won. Half way through this there's a knock at the door. George opens it and the Irish porter bursts in. Picture the scene. Miss World is sat up in bed, there's ten thousand pounds spread out all over it and the porter is bearing the best champagne in the house. And as the porter takes a tip from George he says: 'There's one thing I've always wanted to ask you, George. Why did your life go so wrong!'"

As David finished I could just picture George's eyes twinkling as he told the story himself. A touch of Irish and a touch of magic. But despite the humour of the story, there's pathos in it too. Because, unfortunately, it's what people believe that's important. Often the truth of a situation is secondary.

I know that when I left Liverpool people had written me off. Maybe I was not right for them at the time, I'm not going to argue with that, but I know that some people *believed* I was over the hill. They didn't look at the facts like my age, my fitness, my lack of injury. They just jumped to conclusions and that was that.

I tell you now, Wolverhampton Wanderers got the best bargain of their history when they bought me. I was so determined to do well that I was worth ten men. Within a couple of seasons we'd won the League Cup, had been in Europe and had been in the semi-finals of the FA Cup. When I went up to collect the League Cup, every step up to the royal box I was thinking: "Take that ———, write me off would you, take that ———". I'm not going to mention names, but they know who they are.

But back to the point. That the public's view is important, and takes some changing, is a theme David developed when he spotted Frank Bruno's name on my list.

"A lovely man," David announced. "And a lot more clever than some people give him credit for. I believe he's developing into a real character, somebody who will be able to fill the shoes of Henry Cooper one day.

"Take the famous 'Where's Harry?' business after the Bugner fight. He knew only too well the fight was exclusive to ITV and that Harry Carpenter couldn't interview him at ringside. But it made everybody laugh and was one more story to add to the growing legend. He's not going to be an undisputed world champion with the boxers we've got around at the moment. But Terry Lawless, his manager, must take credit for Frank's maturing. He's certainly right for inclusion in any list of current Great Britons, and my guess is you'll still be talking about him in ten years' time."

As David and I talked it became clear that he and I shared the same feeling about the way to define a "Great" Briton. Record books alone could not determine it. There had to be something more. But what of another man on my list, who not only had all the extra special ingredients but could also probably fill ten pages of this book with lists of his achievements? I'm talking about David Bryant, the recognised master of national and international bowls.

Mention of this name set David Coleman thinking. "It's a long time since I did my first interview with him," he explained. "It was at the 1962 Commonwealth Games. I had a day off from the track and field and decided to go and watch the bowls for a change. I met David Bryant and was so impressed both by his play and by his manner that I did a piece on him. I remember he was very pleased because he was concerned that bowls wasn't getting the coverage it deserved.

"Since then David has rectified that situation almost single-handedly. And I'm very pleased to see that he's still playing, and winning, and able to enjoy the benefits of the new popularity of bowls. He's a must in any list of Great Britons; he qualifies on every count."

It struck me that David Bryant and, for example, Mike Gatting were worlds apart. I suggested this to David.

"Not so," he said, looking at my list. "You know there's at least one common factor in all these people, a will to win, an inner determination. It won't always be obvious in people like David Bryant and Sandy Lyle. But in others such as Nora Perry and Sean Kerly, it's up front. Take Sandy for example, he's one of the most relaxed and easy-going people I know. His natural character is like that, so it's not hard for him to take it onto the golf course with him. But make no mistake about it, without the determination he'd be an also ran. It's got to be there.

"Nora, on the other hand, is bristling with her will to win, almost as if she's nursed some injured pride and now wants to take it out on her opponents. It's plain for all to see, but that doesn't make her better, or worse of course, than sportsmen like Sandy. Hidden or not, I'd say that a fierce determination is a strong linking factor amongst your 'greats'."

At this point David picked up my list and took a long hard look at it.

"I was just about to make some more generalisations, but with people like Steve Davis there, that's very hard." What did he mean?

"To my mind Steve is a bit of a mystery man. I know that some people think he's a bit dull, but there's a lot more to him than meets the eye. He's one of our truly great champions, unrivalled master of a very competitive sport. If you can get to what makes Steve tick, then I suspect you've got one up on the psychologists. He's genial, yet very determined. He obviously loves winning but shows little difference in emotion whether he's just won the World Championship or just lost it – and he's done both in pretty remarkable circumstances. That should be an interesting conversation. My only tip is, Emlyn, knowing what you're like, don't challenge him to a game of snooker. And if you do, don't put money on it!"

I was just about to offer David some side interest in a Hughes versus Davis clash when he came up with one more point about Steve.

"I should say that, in common with so many of your chosen band, I think Steve really gets a thrill out of playing his sport. When he's on the table he's doing something he loves; it's not really work for him."

The more David talked the more I realised that he and I spoke the same language. We recognised the same qualities in the sports men and women we were discussing. I had decided not to embarrass David by including him as one of my list simply because I wanted his help and advice rather than a straight interview. But there's no doubt that he is one of the Great Britons of sport. His knowledge and experience are immense. Most of all, he loves sport.

I'll tell anybody that's prepared to listen that a life in sport is the best you can hope for. I've never known any other and I haven't regretted a single minute of my time. There have been moments that I'd rather not think about too often, but I'd never change them. Not winning the treble in 1977 – we'd won the League, the European Cup and lost in the FA Cup

Final to Manchester United – was a bitter blow. But I'm not sorry. And although I don't think it will be done, it's still there to aim for.

Cups and trophies aside, however, sport is about people, friendships and togetherness. I know that David shares my view that sport can be the best bridge-builder, the most wonderful international language that ever existed. There are people around who make a living *out of* sport, and people who make a living *in* sport. There's a difference. David is of the second type. He's prepared to put back into sport something of the rewards he's had from it. He's also happy to use his influence for good, whenever possible. Thinking along these lines, we came to the name of Virginia Wade.

"I was doing a Sports Aid Foundation event at the Serpentine in London," David explained. "Barclays Bank, I think (if not, perhaps they'd like to do it!) were offering some sports stars £500 apiece to jump into the Serpentine – not a lot of fun on a winter's morning. There was Goochie, Roger Black, Liz Hobbs, Kathy Taylor and a few others. Just before the dreadful moment, Ginny turns up. She's just flown in from Australia and saw the date in her diary. So she jumps in a cab and comes over. Within minutes she's arguing with the organisers because they say they can't find a swimming suit for her. She would have done it, and probably caught pneumonia at the same time.

"She's a lovely girl and always happy to help. In fact," David glanced at my list again, "I don't think there's a name on there that I couldn't ask to attend an event. That's one of the strengths of sport, and we mustn't forget it. We talked earlier about Botham, but you can't ever take away from him the million or so pounds he's collected for leukaemia research. And Besty too, the most generous lad ever, although don't rely on him to turn up!"

Bridge-building between nations and helping out others. You don't need to look any further down my list than my pal Her Royal Highness The Princess Royal. Princess Anne, as I think I'll always know her, surely does more than anybody with her tireless work for the Save the Children Fund, Riding for the Disabled and a host of other charities. In a word, magic. I mentioned her name to David, interested in his response.

"She doesn't need to use sport as a means of getting her name known and doing the work for charity. I believe she's got some useful family connections! But what she does do is use her love of sport as a way to break down any barriers that may exist. I've been in her company on a number of occasions and I know she's most relaxed, most happy, when she's talking about sport. And don't be mistaken, she takes it all very seriously. To be able to compete, and win, at eventing, steeplechasing and flat racing is no small achievement."

David's daughter, Anne, had represented Great Britain juniors at show jumping and I wondered if the two Annes' careers had overlapped at any stage.

"We used to see Her Royal Highness at events and I'd sometimes get a chance to talk to her in the collecting ring. What I did notice was that she was never given the credit she deserved for working with horses that weren't the best. I think we all assumed that there was a bit of money available and that she could go out and buy the best in the market. But to my knowledge she never did. Her horse Doublet was, I've been told, something of an error in breeding. I'm not totally certain of that, but you could tell from the horse that it wasn't from the top flight. And Goodwill must have been related to a camel. But she made the best of the horses.

"I actually believe that she could still win events, three-day or just jumping, today if she had the right horse. Princess Anne," (David, too, used her popular name), "is a bit special. But I don't need to tell you that, Emlyn."

No, David. You don't. I have to say that David first introduced me to the lovely lady and for that, and a lot of other things, I'm eternally grateful.

Our discussion about Her Royal Highness had included a mention of David's daughter. I knew that, however modest David might be about his own achievements in sport and sports commentating, he wasn't backward in coming forward when it came to talking about his children. The only person I know who's worse is that proud father, Emlyn Hughes.

Because the *A Question of Sport* shows are recorded on a Sunday I often take Barbara, my wife, and Emma and Emlyn, our children, along. Being away from home for most of the week means I don't get enough time to spend with the family. Before a recording we have a bite to eat and there's a chance to chat to the guests. Emma and Emlyn are selective autograph hunters. They want some people to sign a book or a photograph, but not others. It can be quite amusing to see them ask somebody like Stephen Hendry (Emma's a great fan) or Glen Hoddle (one of Emlyn's heroes) but not another guest who may be standing next to them. They're forbidden, of course, to ask Peter Reid, Kevin Sheedy, or any of the other Everton lads who have been on the show.

At these pre-recording get-togethers the BBC always looks after us very well, and David, in particular, takes great delight in being as cheeky as possible towards Emma. I think he has a soft spot for her; I know he can make her blush at the drop of a hat. David's own daughter Anne was, and is, a very successful horsewoman, show jumping being her speciality. When she represented Great Britain at the European Junior Championships it was as a team mate of a certain John Francome.

12

"Because I knew John's family from those early days of trekking round the shows I've always felt a keen interest in his development. I remember that the BBC cameras were present at his first National Hunt meeting. I suggested that we took some footage of him that day as it might be a little piece of history in years to come. I wouldn't swear now that I thought he would go on to win seven jockeys' championships but I always thought he was a bit special."

As David said this I remembered that more than one friend from the world of riding had said that, in their opinion, John's greatest asset was his ability to present a horse to a fence. You'd never see a horse of John's wrong-footed on its approach. I mentioned this to David.

"I agree. And I'm sure that the show jumping background has a lot to do with that. Apart from all his supreme ability, John is a lovely man. In fact, Emlyn, your list is full of them. People like Nigel Mansell, John Lowe, Gareth Edwards and Sebastian Coe. They are all great champions and also all great people."

This comment from David raised a question I wanted to put to him. I knew that what he said was true, but that wasn't always the picture that emerged in the press. Take, for example, Princess Anne. She was hardly overburdened with praise from the press when she was at the height of her sporting success. Nigel Mansell, too, is sometimes thought to be irritable and a little bit difficult, although I know him to be a very giving and kind man.

"Nigel is a classic example," David said. "You're right in what you say. I can remember Nigel giving us an interview from his bedroom in Monte Carlo when he had a room full of guests waiting to take him out to dinner. He had stood in for James Hunt at the last minute. But Nigel can sometimes appear short-tempered if reporters or autograph hunters try to get to him just before a race. He's about to risk his life, and the lives of others, at 200 miles per hour, and some fool reporter wants to know his views on some newspaper tittle-tattle.

"Princess Anne is another example. She used to have to put up with flash bulbs and a hum of conversation when she was taking her horse through the dressage stage of an event, a challenge for rider and horse that demands absolute attention and concentration. In my opinion her occasional outbursts were quite restrained."

"My real worry, David," I explained, "is that the stars I'm talking to will treat me as a reporter or journalist. I don't want that to affect our relationship."

"I'm sure it won't, in your case, but I know what you mean. The press have been responsible for a lot of bad news about sport, and not always a lot of good news. As we all know, they want to make you a superstar overnight, and then when you've made it, they're quick to knock you down.

"Take a chap like John Lowe who I see is on your list. You couldn't wish to meet a nicer guy, but he's very much his own man. And that hasn't always endeared him to the media. I remember when the world championships used to be held at Jollys in Stoke. John would always go home after the evening so you couldn't find him in the bar; this kind of thing would eventually annoy some members of the press and so they'd invent stories. It's a kind of gossip really."

So how has David managed to retain such a respected position within British sport over the countless years he's been reporting it? I think the answer lies in his ability to listen and only contribute when asked.

Take football as a prime example. When I was at Liverpool never a day went past without somebody telling me how to do my job better. Had I been a doctor I can't imagine these same people coming up to me and telling me what pills to prescribe or that the diagnosis I made last week was wrong. Do lorry drivers get people stopping them in pubs and telling them that they're changing gear too soon or not turning right correctly? Of course not. But as public entertainers you have to expect to take a bit more of that – but not from the press. I wouldn't think to pick up a reporter on his spelling or the way he phrased his last article, although sometimes a bit of criticism would be valuable.

This story of David's epitomises his attitude to his job, and says a lot about the qualities of Sebastian Coe too. David told me this when discussing the role of the media in sports reporting.

"After Seb's disastrous run in the Moscow 800 metres in 1980 I was speaking to my friend Brendan Foster. I said that Seb had spoilt his race by not getting involved and by never really competing. I also pointed out that he shouldn't get too despondent – one didn't become a bad athlete in a week. He still had the 1500 metres to go for and he should be getting ready for that.

"Brendan told me to go and tell Seb that. It would be just the right kind of advice at the time. I didn't feel I could. It wasn't my business.

"Anyway, I had decided to do nothing when I spotted Seb in the car park outside the stadium in Moscow. He came straight over to me and said that Brendan had told him that I had something to say to him. What was it? Of course, I couldn't do anything else so I told him. Seb thanked me warmly for my advice and, as we all know, went out and won the 1500 metres by fighting all the way round. That, for me, sums up the role of the reporter, whether it's for a paper or broadcasting. I do remember being able to use the line about not becoming a bad athlete in a week as Seb burst over the line in his famous 1500 metres victory."

As we spoke about Seb Coe, David pointed out that I had another great athlete on my list, although he was probably there for his rugby achievements. Gareth Edwards was, in David's opinion, one of the best all-round athletes he had seen in his years of reporting sport.

"You'll probably know," David said, "that Gareth's greatest thrill when leaving rugby was to sign on for Swansea City, then under the management of John Toshak. Tosh knew that he was unlikely ever to play Gareth but the little man kept pestering and nagging him for a game. He just wanted to pull on that white jersey and be a 'Swan'.

"Eventually John relented and put Gareth on the wing for a reserve match at Bournemouth. In the first half nothing much happened, mostly because nobody passed the ball to Gareth; Gareth thinks his team mates had orders from the boss! Anyway, in the second half Gareth gets the ball and is heavily tackled by a young full back. As the two get up from the ground, in front of a crowd of two men and a dog, the youngster speaks to Gareth. 'You don't remember me, do you sir?' Gareth looks at him for a moment and realises this was a young man that Gareth used to teach at college! It was all too much for him and I don't think Gareth has played since."

When I spoke to Gareth I knew I would be able to share my retirement story with him. I was playing for Rotherham one day and a youngster got the ball in front of me, pulled it down, feigned to go one way and actually went the other. It was a neat piece of play, but the sad thing for me was that I knew he was going to do it. . .and I couldn't stop him. At that moment I knew I had to quit. I think I played a few more games, but I knew it was over. I'm not sorry, and I'm relieved that I saw the signs. I suppose Frank Worthington will retire one day, but probably not yet.

David and I chatted on about sport, about our lives in sport and the people we had met. I was tempted to ask David what he thought were the common characteristics among the stars on my list. But I also wanted to make my own mind up. I decided to compromise and ask him for one thing he thought all top sports stars had in common. After that, I would do my own investigation. David found no hesitation in coming up with his answer.

"In a word, competitiveness," he announced. "One of the best pieces of advice I ever received was not to play cards with professional sports men and women. They have to win. I would extend that advice to snakes and ladders, Trivial Pursuit, draughts, chess, the puzzle your child gets in the Christmas cracker, in fact anything at which there can be a winner."

Having just come from a game of tennis with Colin Bell, the ex-Manchester City and England inside-forward, I had to agree. A friendly? Some joke. No two people ever put more effort and determination (we won't mention skill) into a tennis match. We are great friends, but we both wanted to win. I knew what David meant.

So, with that summing up and piece of advice, I had to thank David Coleman for his help and prepare myself for the interviews ahead. And, in case you want to know, I beat Colin 6–2, 6–2. Me? Competitive?

Gareth Edwards

where the grass is greener

Gareth Owen Edwards was born in July 1947 at Gwaen-cae-Gurwen. He made his debut for Wales in 1967 after playing club rugby for Cardiff. Edwards played fifty-three times in succession for Wales, during which time they won seven international championships, five Triple Crowns and two Grand Slams. At the age of twenty years and seven months, he became the youngest captain of Wales. An MBE in 1975 crowned a great career, and he retired in 1978 having had the distinction of scoring more tries than any other scrum-half in world rugby.

The story of Gareth Edwards is, of course, a sad one for sport. That's because it's a story of missed opportunities and of what might have been. And if you think I'm talking nonsense, you only have to check the record books.

Gareth Edwards was just sixteen when he was picked to play for the under-eighteen West Wales Youth soccer team. As a result of his performance he was asked to sign forms for Swansea Town – and this offer was the first of several from professional clubs. I wonder if Gareth would have been a part of my pal John Toshak's plans as he took Swansea City (as they were later known) from the Fourth to the First Division in the late seventies and early eighties. But it was not to be; the offer was declined and the soccer career that might have been was nipped in the bud. And in athletics, too, Gareth was on the threshold of an international career. As a schoolboy he held the United Kingdom record for the 200 yards low hurdles and also gained international representative honours at this level. But, unfortunately, he didn't graduate to the senior level and we are left to ponder on what might have been achieved.

Why was it then, that a young man so gifted in both soccer and athletics failed to make the grade in either? The answer is simple, and well known. Gareth Edwards could not be expected to find the time for other sports as he was in the process of becoming a legend in Welsh rugby. He became the country's most capped player and will always be remembered as the most brilliant scrum-half in an era when the Welsh side dominated international rugby and where brilliance was not the exception but the order of the day. Perhaps soccer players and athletes of his generation ought to be grateful that rugby claimed the man. Having said that, if he had turned up at Anfield and tried any of those jinking runs that he tells me were his hallmark as a left-winger, I'm pretty sure that Tommy Smith would have found a way of dealing with him. In fact Gareth might have felt he was playing rugby with the kind of tackle Tommo would have put in!

The fact that Gareth was going to achieve something in sport was quite clear from a young age. He even told his Dad that one day he was going to play for Wales, although neither Gareth nor his father can remember which sport he was referring to at the time. On the subject of international honours, a further check of the record books will reveal an interesting fact. Gareth's schoolboy international debut as an athlete was in the England team! This was because he had won through to selection representing Millfield, an English school. Although mentioning the word "England" can get you thrown out of some Welsh valleys, it seems that Gareth has been forgiven for what must be regarded as a minor aberration of his youth.

So what was it that made Gareth such an outstanding sportsman at a young age? Where better to ask the man than in the heart of the valleys, at Glynneath? I should explain that the venue for our meeting was the Glynneath Golf Club, but the less said about our achievements in that particular sport the better. Not even Gareth can claim a lost international career in golf!

"When I was young," Gareth explained, "sport was what you did when you weren't at school. You didn't watch television, play computer games or go to discos. You played sport. It didn't really matter what season it was either, it was just rugby, soccer or cricket depending on what kind of ball you could get hold of. And it certainly didn't matter what time of day it was. We just played until we got told to come in at night. My mother would occasionally shout out to me to come in but I took no notice. Even my father calling out made no difference, especially when I was about to score a match-saving try. It was only when my father strode out the front of the house and told me that I had one minute to get in, or else, that I knew the final whistle had sounded for me."

Listening to Gareth, "Gags" as I've always known him, reminded me of so many other sport stars of my generation and before. As kids, these stars thought of nothing else but playing sport. In some cases they were simply obsessive about one sport, but for most of them there was nothing else to do anyway. I'm not sorry that the youth of today have so many more opportunities, but I think it's unrealistic to hope that another Gareth Edwards or George Best is simply going to appear out of nowhere. The stars of tomorrow are probably sat at home watching a video right now. They're going to need encouragement and coaching.

Of course, playing to all hours is no guarantee of success, although it certainly helps. More is needed; it might be a touch of genius, a lucky break or forceful parents. In Gareth's case it was his association with one man, his school teacher and rugby advisor, Bill Samuel. Now I had heard about Bill before. Gareth speaks so highly of him in his autobiography and is never slow to acknowledge the importance of Samuel's guiding hand in his career. But it raised a laugh when I asked Gareth about his "advisor".

"He never 'advised' me, just told me what I was going to do. He would make announcements like 'you'll never be a centre, scrum-half for you' and 'you'd better go and play for Swansea now, I'll tell them you're going to play for Wales one day'. Sometimes I resented his attitude to me but I think, deep down, I always knew he was doing things for the best. And he knew his rugby; he was a very talented coach.

"Not all of his pronouncements came true, like playing for Swansea for example, but he never gave up. I think that his determination won me my place at Millfield School, and that was a very important step for me."

Important? I would have thought it was quite a shock for the young boy from the valleys to go to one of the most prestigious and expensive public schools in England. I wanted to ask Gareth about it, but didn't want to suggest that he had any reason to feel out of place there. I tried the famous Hughes' tactful approach – guaranteed to offend.

"Gags, you must have felt a little. . ." (what was the word I wanted?) "a little. . .overawed." Yes, that's it.

"What, because I was poor and everyone else was rich?" Gareth put it in a nutshell. "The honest answer is no. At one point there were six of us in one room, five sons of millionaires and me. Back home I would even wear some of the clothes that the richer lads had thrown out. But the beauty of the school was that money was not made to be an important topic. Achieving what you were capable of, whether sporting or academic, was what mattered to the headmaster, 'Boss' Meyer.

"In fact he once told me not to look down on the other boys at the school just because I was better than them at rugby; they didn't look down on me because I was a miner's son."

"Going back to your question, Em," Gareth continued, "you will probably understand what I mean about never feeling inferior. What people earned and what kind of house they lived in was not important to me as a youngster. I've read in books and magazines that I came from a poor background. But I never thought of it like that. Dad was a miner and had to work hard; however, we never really wanted for anything. We were like everyone else in the valley and there was pride in being in work and turning up for chapel in decent clothes and so on. So, although I knew my parents couldn't possibly have afforded the Millfield fees, I never felt ill at ease there."

That is one of the great strengths of sport. Ability is what counts. Billy Bremner, the captain of the great Leeds United side in the sixties and seventies, was once told he was too small for professional football. Happily he proved the truth of the old saying: "if you're good enough, you're big enough". The same goes for your background. If you're good enough, you're rich enough. And there was never a question mark over Gareth's ability to make the grade.

The Millfield fees were paid by scholarship, an arrangement that Bill Samuel engineered by his numerous letters and calls to the school about his protégé, Gareth Edwards. It must have been quite something for the lad from Gwaen-cae-Gurwen, Gareth's village, to attend a school like that. I began to wonder if it had affected his attitude to home life at all. I had always known Gareth as a modest man, but he did have something to boast about when he was young. Had it been hard for him to retain his sense of values?

"I expect I was a bit unbearable at times," Gareth admitted, "but more because of my sporting achievements than because of the school I went to. The lads in Gwaen-cae-Gurwen wouldn't have been impressed by the fact that I went to Millfield. It was only a school after all. But playing for the Welsh Secondary Schools XV, as I did a couple of times, would have made me something out of the ordinary. To be quite honest, I don't think I changed much, not then and not until this day."

"But you must have been growing in confidence," I suggested, "what with the backing of the school and the honours that kept coming your way."

"That's an interesting one. The funny thing is I've never been that confident of my own ability. I always expected to get picked, knew I was worth a place and was disappointed if not in the team. But once the game came around I was a bundle of nerves, worrying about if I would drop the ball at the crucial moment or miss the vital pass. Some players seem to take it all in their stride but I found that the higher I went in the game, the more anxious I became. My stomach would be churning and I would feel unable to join in much of the pre-match banter. But, like most sportsmen I know, once the game started I forgot about nerves and just got on with it."

I could understand exactly how Gareth felt. In fact, as Gareth talked, I began to realise some of the similarities between him and me. Perhaps this is part of the reason we get on so well together. We have both captained our countries and have both been part of a team that was reckoned, at the time, to be extra special. On the personal side, we both enjoy family life to the full. I wondered if our attitude to our sports was the same.

"When I was young Gareth, I used to want to play for England, win an FA Cup Final, play in the World Cup and everything else that was going. Without boasting, I have to say that I did all that, and yet I still had ambitions; there were still things I wanted to achieve in soccer.

"Was it the same for you in rugby?" I asked. "You had achieved your ambition of playing for Wales, you had won more caps than anyone else, had won a series in New Zealand with The Lions, had captained your country. . .what more was there for you?" I wondered if Gareth's ambition was the same as mine. It was:

"All I wanted us to do was to achieve what I knew we were capable of. I wanted Wales not just to win, but to win in style. I wanted us to go out there on the park and give the opposition such a performance that they never got near the ball, never even sniffed it. There were many games that we knew we could win; with a bit of huff and puff we could make the match safe. But I wanted us to cream the other team, give them and the crowd such an exhibition that they would always remember us as the greatest side around."

"Did it ever happen?"

"No. But we sometimes got near. What about you Em?"

"It was just the same for me at Liverpool. We knew we were the best and could win matches. When I first played for 'Pool that's all I wanted; as long as we won I didn't care how. But as I played more I realised that the way in which you won was important."

Thinking about it later, I suppose that's the beauty of the thing, what keeps top performers in every sport going. Sport is about competing and winning; but winning is not everything and never can be. If you can do it – do it in style. Mind you, if I follow that advice I could be playing golf until I'm a hundred. "And the rest" did someone say?

Apart from this business of winning in style, are there other similarities between Gareth and me? I suspected, for example, that he had the same attitude to authority as I did.

"My approach," said Gareth thoughtfully, "was based on the fact that 'they' were always going to be there. They might be selectors, coaches, referees, administrators, or even groundsmen. . .but if they had a bit of authority they might decide to use it. In these circumstances I always thought it best to be as nice as possible. Be diplomatic. If they can put one over on the captain of Wales it can keep them happy for weeks; but what good does it do me to prove a point to some petty official whom I'm never going to see again – if I can possibly help it? To be fair, though, most people in rugby put in such a lot of unpaid work that the last thing they need is some international player trying to throw his weight around. Live and let live must be my motto."

"And does the same go for the press?"

"Now that's a different story." By the look on Gareth's face it might mean this book suddenly gets an "18" rating. "To put the record straight, most of the press are doing a job and good luck to them. But some of them deserve to be banned from rugby grounds for life. They haven't played the game, they don't understand the game and, what's worse, they don't seem to care about the game. I'm not going to be too specific but their criticisms can be so destructive and hurtful. What they seem to forget is that people play rugby for pleasure. It's competitive, hard and international honour can be at stake – but nobody gets paid for doing it. Reporters get paid to say unkind and untruthful things about people who are unable to hit back. It's only because I'm retired from the game that I can say this – and this is only a mild reproach. How would reporters feel if we wrote about all the times they spelled a player's name incorrectly or every time they got their grammar wrong?"

Enough said, Gareth. It could have been me talking. But like so many things in sport, the few spoil it for the rest. Listening to Gareth talk about the press reminded me of one aspect of our careers that could never be the same. I got paid for playing football; Gareth could never take a penny. I asked if it irritated him.

"No, Em. But it reminds me that you'd better pay for the next round!"

While I did as I was told a couple of local rugby fans (they couldn't have been golf fans) asked Gareth for an autograph. These two chaps, looking a trifle the worse for wear, thanked Gareth for the autograph and then began chatting to him about a match in which Gareth had played for Cardiff some nine or ten years previously. When they'd gone Gareth pointed after them.

"You see," he explains, "that's what it's all about, being a rugby player in Wales. You belong to the people. They expect you to train like a marine, have the dedication of a monk and play like a bloody magician and then still have six pints with the lads on Saturday night and never mind the airs and graces. And I wouldn't have it any other way! I can't say I don't like the nice hotels when we've been on tour, and I'm not going to turn my nose up at a free meal and a drink from time to time, but rugby is an amateur sport and that's the way it ought to stay.

"I've had large offers from rugby league clubs. Those boys, more than once, have unrolled large bundles of notes under my nose, just to tempt me like. And I'm grateful and flattered. But I'm never going to leave home, the valleys, and the people around these parts."

"So what was it that tempted you to leave the game so early? You seemed to give up when you still had a year or more in you."

"It's a story I've told in my autobiography but I'm happy to tell it again. I had been thinking about packing up for some time but this one match, against Ireland at Lansdowne Road, sealed it for me.

"The game proved a number of things to me. First, I realised that being Welsh gave you no divine right to win. You had to work hard for every ball and every point. I had been part of a team that had set new standards but that was yesterday, the last match. You couldn't rest on your laurels because next week or next season there would be new challenges. Second, I think I realised that we would never be able to go out and win as convincingly and well as I wanted. We won that day but it was such a struggle. And third, the game drained me so much, physically and emotionally, that I recognised that my time was running out and I had better quit while I was still able to be proud of my performance.

"On the day we were struggling against such a determined Irish side that

I can only compare it with swimming against the tide and feeling ready to give in and drown. No matter how hard we tried we could not push them back. At 13–13 we could lose the match and our chances of the Triple Crown and Grand Slam. And then it happened, with four minutes to go, a decent ball, a bit of magic, and the game was won. I knew, however, that I never wanted to go through it all again. We had beaten the Irish and, for my part at least, they could stay beaten.

"I did play twice more for Wales, completing the season and sweeping the honours. But if ever I had second thoughts, a fan's greeting after my last match clinched it: 'Australia next, Gareth, then New Zealand, and try and get South Africa so we'll be champions of the world!' Even thinking about it was too exhausting."

So that was the end of Gareth's career, a man who had done so much for British sport not only through his outstanding ability, but also through his modest, charming and quietly inspiring manner. There only remains the question that many may wish to ask: "Where is he now?"

Followers of A Question of Sport may recall Gareth as my first adversary on the programme. He was also involved in rugby commentaries on both television and radio. Gareth confessed to enjoying the excitement and the performance of broadcasting but, perhaps like his soccer and athletics "careers", this was not to be. For Gareth has developed the many business interests that he was following while playing rugby and today is a director of several companies. What with this work, numerous public appearances in and around his native South Wales, his golf and fishing and time spent with his family, there's not much time left. . .just enough, in fact, for those few pints on a Saturday night down at the club with the other lads from the valley.

Sandy Lyle

the confidence that counts

Sandy Lyle, son of a professional golfer, has worked his way to the top with a series of increasingly impressive successes. The reward for his years of experience on both the European and American circuits came with his victory in the 1985 British Open – the first for a home golfer since Tony Jacklin. This was followed by an important role in the two European successes in the Ryder Cup against America in 1985 and 1987. Most recently he has added another "major" to his haul by winning the 1988 US Masters title in Augusta. Although born in England, having Scottish parents has enabled him to represent that country in international golf.

*L*ooking confident, fit and happy, Sandy Lyle met me at his lovely home just by the Sunningdale Golf Course. The sun was shining on the well-kept lawns, just as it was shining on the fortunes of the thirty-year-old golfer. He had every reason to be happy, having just come back from the United States with the famous green jacket that goes with winning the US Masters Championship in his luggage. The confidence and fitness clearly flowed from this victory. For golf, probably more than any other game, is one when the mind and the body have to be in tune.

Feeling fit can help your shots. Playing good golf does your sense of well-being no harm at all. But Sandy, as one of the most feared professionals in the game, and I, one of the least feared but most devoted amateurs around, both know that success at golf is very elusive. Without wishing to compare myself in any way with Sandy, I told him about my recent exploits. Six weeks without a match at all was the lead-up to a pro–am I played two weeks before our interview. I went into it hoping to get under a ton-fifteen and emerged the winner with a round of ninety. The next weekend, however, feeling full of myself on account of the previous result, I missed my 115 by just one shot. There's no answer to that – that is golf. But was it the same for professionals as amateurs? Did Sandy fear a switch in form as dramatic, in his terms, as mine?

"At the moment I'm feeling good of course. I'm in the middle of a short holiday, I've just recorded one of the most important victories of my career and my fitness is everything I wish it to be. If I got out into a tournament tomorrow I'd hope to do well. That's not to say, however, that I wouldn't feel the need to prepare for it thoroughly, just that my confidence is high and so I'd approach the course and the competition in a very positive frame of mind.

"But your game can go, just overnight sometimes," he added.

"Has that been your experience?" I asked.

"Not often. I've tended to have periods in the doldrums and times when I've been playing well. In general terms, however, my career has been one of steady progress."

I was interested to hear Sandy confirm this view of his progress in golf. I could hear Peter Alliss saying, many years ago, that Sandy Lyle was a golfer of great promise. This was a point he repeated over a period of years. I'm sure I wasn't alone in wondering whether Sandy would ever realise that potential. Perhaps we'd all become so used to the overnight success story that we'd grown impatient with somebody like Sandy who took his time learning the game and, importantly, learning how to win. But there's no mistaking the fact that once Sandy got the hang of winning it became something of a habit.

I asked Sandy about his progression. Had it been a long, slow haul?

"In some ways you could say that, since I started playing when I was three! My father was the professional and greenkeeper at Hawkstone Park, near Shrewsbury. He had moved down from Scotland to take up the post. There was a forty-bedroom hotel, a swimming pool and the golf course. My bedroom, when I was a child, looked out over the practice ground.

"It seemed to me to be very natural to play golf. I've got a photograph of me at the age of about three or four, holding a club and wearing wellington boots."

"Did your father push you at all?"

"I don't think 'push' is quite right. But he certainly encouraged me, and also criticised me. After every round I played we'd have a post mortem. He'd go over shots I'd missed and go through what he saw as the weaker parts of my game. What sometimes upset me was when he'd go over rounds I'd played that he hadn't seen. When I got home he'd ask what my score was and then ask how I could have improved on it.

"However, when it came time for me to choose some sort of career, he never pushed golf. Obviously it was an option, but he made it quite clear that he would support me in whatever occupation I wanted to follow."

One similarity between my situation and Sandy's was having a father involved professionally in sport. My father was keen for each of his three sons to make a go of it in pro sport. Apart from my own achievements, one of my brothers played rugby league for a while and the other dabbled in soccer, actually being on Liverpool's books for a short time. In football it was clear whether you had a chance or not by the strength of interest being shown in you by the clubs. In golf, however, the situation is not like that. It's very much an individual game, and the decision to take it up professionally must be a hard one. Perhaps the only way of judging the likelihood of success is by looking at your own record of achievement. I asked Sandy about his progress as a young player.

"I was playing off three when I was thirteen and could regularly score below par by the time I was fifteen. Naturally this gave me great encouragement. What spurred me on most of all were the opportunities to travel that started coming my way when I was about sixteen or so. There's nothing like travel for exciting the imagination, and I enjoyed my trips to amateur tournaments and as an English youth player."

I was surprised to hear that Sandy had played for England as a youth. Although I knew he hadn't been born in Scotland I always thought that it was Scottish blood that coursed through his veins. The idea of a Jock representing England takes some getting used to.

"I actually played golf for England as a youth and for Scotland, on account of my parents' birthplace, as a senior. I think the rules have been changed to stop anybody representing both countries. I don't mind really whether I'm classed as English, Scottish or just British most of the time. Of course, in golf terms, the important division is between American and European."

I think I can forgive him his odd decision to represent Scotland, providing he keeps up his winning ways when playing against the Americans in the Ryder Cup. Regardless of nationality, I wanted to take Sandy back to the period between deciding to try his luck as a golfer and the recent heady days when every tournament seems to be there for his taking. I reminded him of Peter Alliss's assessment using, I think, Peter's own words.

"Peter used to say that you were about to 'burst onto the scene'. Instead, your career has steadily flowed. How do you explain this?"

"I suppose I found it hard to win things for the first time. But more than that, I just took time over learning the craft. Since starting on the circuit I've matured a great deal. I'm able to deal with pressure a lot better and I've also cut out a lot of mistakes. Perhaps that's the key to long-term success. If you're playing well then carry on; don't think about it, let it all flow naturally. If you're playing badly, minimise the damage by taking extra care and cutting out as many mistakes as possible.

"I also think that I'm about the right age now. I'm mentally strong as well as being physically capable. With the American tour you do have to be strong. Playing regularly, often in hot weather, can be quite demanding. I'm about thirteen stone right now which is just right for me. I was much larger at one time. Cutting down a little on drink has actually made a difference in this respect." This last comment was greeted by a shout of "just one a day" from the adjoining room.

The comment on Sandy's drinking came from his Dutch girlfriend Jolande. I had actually read about her work in sports massage, her speciality apparently being a technique to relieve strains and tension by working on pressure points in the feet. Some rather tongue-in-cheek comments from the golfing press aside, whatever it was she did, it certainly had the right effect. She joined us in the conversation. I mentioned to Sandy about my own approach to drinking. I had recently been converted to a diet of mostly fruit juice and mineral water having found that my lifestyle left me little time to train. Although I had never been a big eater, the combination of a couple of pints of beer each evening and then a few hours sitting in a car the following day was beginning to leave its mark on my waistline. Now it was the juice and water and, if I went to the pub, wine only. In the four months prior to meeting Sandy I had lost a couple of stone and felt great for it.

Sandy had faced exactly the same kind of problem as I had. It wasn't that either of us drank to excess, well not normally, but that a couple of drinks a day had started to mean a gain in weight. Sandy also faced the additional problem of owning a pub; this is just near his home and is managed by his brother-in-law.

Jolande looked on as we spoke. Her help with Sandy's fitness and health, so important over a long tour, had obviously been a contributory factor in his success. I asked if there were others, particularly in his younger days, who had helped him significantly.

"Not apart from my father. He really taught me everything that I didn't learn for myself."

"And later on?" I asked.

"I suppose the one who springs to mind most readily is Jimmy Ballard. He helped me change my swing at a time when I was going through a difficult time. My game didn't seem to be getting any better and I was slipping down the money lists. I had personal problems too. I met Jimmy in Florida where I watched him teaching one or two other professionals. I asked for some advice and within three weeks had won the Tournament Players Championship at Greensboro. That not only boosted my confidence no end but guaranteed me ten years no-qualification entry into tournaments on the US tour.

"Jimmy was amazed that I could change my style so quickly. Today he still helps me; we try to get together a couple of times a year.

"Just as important as people who helped me in the direct sense were those I was able to watch and learn from," Sandy continued.

"Did you have particular favourites?"

"Tony Jacklin I always admired, but I think Gary Player was one of the most influential. He is such a good golfer in the technical sense, but also a great fighter."

I had been privileged to watch Gary at close hand once, and told Sandy about it. It was in a pro–am tournament at Woburn for a glass manufacturer both he and I worked for. The idea was that Gary and I would play a hole and then move on both hole and partner; we therefore played the course and had a chance to meet and chat to all the customers and clients. You can tell from the way it was organised that it was a largely social/business gathering. Golf was the setting, not the main reason for being there. But you couldn't convince Gary Player of this. He played every shot as if it was to win the Open, and on the couple of occasions he made a small error he got very cross with himself. Perhaps I shouldn't have been so surprised since I tend to play every testimonial and charity soccer match as if it's for the FA Cup; I guess that's the professional approach.

Sandy listened to my story, saying that he felt Gary was the complete player. "In fact," he added, "if you talk to Gary today he'll tell you he's still capable of winning big tournaments. Who would disagree with him when he's in the right mood?"

Sandy mentioned Gary's mood. Previously he'd talked about confidence and being in the right frame of mind. The more we spoke the more it became clear just how important the emotions are. You'll only get a chance to go for the top if you've got all the skills, but these alone can never be a guarantee of success in golf.

Thinking about the emotional aspects of the game, I suggested to Sandy that his most famous victory, that in the 1985 British Open, must have been an immense mental strain.

"It was hard being the first Brit to win since Tony, but my golf that week went well and I didn't feel too much pressure actually on the course. It's one of those situations that you'll probably understand. I was looking forward to the Open and thought I had some chance of winning. After a couple of rounds I was clearly one of the favourites. I'm sure I would have gone on playing as if it was just another tournament – except for the attention I got from the media. They really blew up the whole thing and it was then that the pressure started to get to me. I'm not complaining, but simply saying that the strain was much greater because of their build-up.

"Being the first since Tony, the one before him being Henry Cotton, meant a lot to British golf and the British press. I was grateful for all the attention but think it was harder to win than it was, say, for Nick Faldo a couple of years later."

"And do you think you will find it easier to win again, having broken the ice in 1985?"

"I think so. The difficulties only arise after a couple of rounds. If you're one of the leaders – and of course this goes for any tournament, not just the Open – you've always got that bit of extra pressure on you. But having been there and done it, it should be easier. I got a lovely personal letter from Henry Cotton after I'd won the Open, congratulating me and saying that he was sure this wasn't going to be the last Open I'd win. I hope I'll prove his prediction correct."

My experiences at Liverpool always made me think it was easier to win something for the second or third time. Other teams fear you more, and you've learned how to win. Both are important psychological advantages to have.

Sandy had explained that he hoped to win more Opens, indeed more majors around the world, so perhaps the question of his greatest moment was inappropriate – that was still for the future. But I did wonder how he ranked his achievements: the Open, the 1988 Masters victory and the great Ryder Cup wins. Was there one that meant more to him than the others?

"I can't really decide, although the Open was special because it's such a prestigious tournament, being the oldest and so full of tradition. Having said that, winning anything in America always gives an extra thrill because you've achieved something in pure golf terms. There can be no complaints about conditions favouring the home player. I'd like to win the US Open of course, but that's a very difficult one. The championship venue is different each year although it's normally one with tight fairways and small greens. In the past I haven't found the courses to my liking."

"They're the good things then Sandy," I said, "but have there been bad times too?"

"Yes, but not individual events, just periods when things haven't been going so well. The period I've already mentioned, just before meeting Jimmy Ballard, was very bad for me."

"During that time, or any other, were there moments when you thought you would give it all up?"

"No, never. I knew in myself that it was a case of keeping going and searching for the missing ingredient. I've never had any other job so the thought didn't enter my head. What else could I do?"

I knew that Sandy didn't expect an answer to that one, but a man with his charm and manner wouldn't be out of work for long. Sandy always has been known as one of the nice men of sport. And it's good to see that he remains exactly the same as the record books start to fill with his achievements. Success doesn't need to change people. Underneath the relaxed and outgoing personality, however, was there a rebel waiting to get out? I put this to Sandy.

"I was never in trouble at school, always did what I was told, and have enjoyed a good relationship with the administrators in golf. Basically, Emlyn, I'm a good boy."

"But haven't you found that some of the things going on in the game get you angry?" My reason for asking this in particular was because almost every other personality I'd interviewed had some major complaint about the way their sport was run.

"Golf is run very well. There are the odd grumbles, but I think most of the players are too busy worrying about the problems of their own game to get worked up about anything else. Golf is treated with respect by the administrators because it's such an old game. There are many aspects that won't be changed because they've stood the test of time. Also, everybody in the sport still loves a round or two, so there's a common bond between even the most famous players and the most humble administrators."

"But what about the things that go on on the fringes of the game?"

"Well, after winning the Open in particular, the 'phone never stopped ringing. Winning the tournament is the easy part, dealing with everything else takes the energy. But I'm not going to complain. It's the sponsors and the advertisers who put the money in, so they've a right to expect something in return."

As we spoke I found myself entering the Lyle frame of mind. Could this be how he deals with opponents on the course? He gets them so comfortable and relaxed that the fires in them start to go out, leaving the way clear for Sandy. Intentional or not, his aura of confidence and contentment must be a strong weapon to take onto a golf course. On the course, however, there are other strong characters stalking about. What sort of player did he enjoy playing with? Did he prefer the contrasting personality of a Gary Player, or was the happy-go-lucky approach of a Trevino more to his liking?

"I like to relax when I'm playing, and I find I can do this with most players. Trevino, for example, is unpopular with some because of the way he chats and jokes. I don't mind that. Greg Norman is the one I have most trouble with. You never know whether he's going to blow up or not. One bad shot from him and I half expect to see his club flying through the air.

"Don't forget that golf is supposed to be a game. You're playing for money and it's a job too. But I still love to play, and still get a good laugh from it."

"Anything that you recall in particular?" I asked.

"Recently in a pro–am my partner went into the edge of some water. The ball was sitting up, just on the surface, near some stones but on soft mud. I suggested he played it. The poor lad took my advice and tried to chip out as if he was in a bunker. Unfortunately he applied about three times as much power as he needed. There was mud everywhere, sparks flying off the stones and not a sign of the ball. I was about to enquire about it when I saw my playing partner fall to the ground. . .clutching what we in sport call the 'upper groin'. Poleaxed by his own shot! The poor chap couldn't walk for some minutes."

I hope Sandy suggested to his unfortunate partner that his injury, like golf, was a case of mind over matter.

I suppose that the one word that springs to mind if trying to sum up my impression of Sandy would be "relaxed". I wondered at the time of the interview if he would have coped with the Liverpool Football Club school of mental preparation. This involved slapping everybody on the back and saying what good players we all were when we won, and then slagging everybody off and blaming the entire world apart from yourself when we lost. In bare outline that's exactly what happened, but I must say that Shanks had a much greater understanding of the psychology of sport than some people might give him credit for. It was a kind of homespun philosophy, but it was carefully thought out and it did work.

Of course, I was interviewing Sandy following some remarkable victories and some great golf. Would he have appeared so in control if he had just returned from a string of defeats and a number of poor performances? I wasn't going to be so rude as to ask him that, but I was interested in his approach to practice if things weren't going so well. I was again reminded of Bill Shankly. His policy was to encourage players to keep up the work on their strengths. He'd say: "If you've got a good right peg, practise with it son, it's that what got you here in the first place." I think his idea was to give the player back some confidence by concentrating, at first, on the good points. The problem areas can follow, but let's get the working parts tuned first. Was this the same for Sandy?

"I know it sounds obvious, but you can't afford to have too many weak points to your game. You must practise everything, because you never know what you're going to need out on the course. Sometimes a course favours a big hitter or a tight putter, but generally you'll be found out if you've got a weakness or two lying in your bag."

What Sandy had in his bag was an extra club marked "confidence". Having met him and talked about his game at some length I was going to watch his future progress with considerable interest. In particular I would be looking for the times when Sandy reached in and drew out that extra club. I had the feeling it was going to be a very useful tool in the months ahead, one that might well bring in a few more "majors" to adorn the walls of his beautiful home. And if Sandy was happy with that, perhaps he could spare Jolande to give me the foot massage. That was something definitely missing from my game.

David Bryant

the perpetual champion

The man with the pipe, David Bryant is probably one of the best known bowlers in the country. The fifty-six-year-old ex-teacher from Avon has won every title in his sport. Outdoors he has been four times Commonwealth Games singles gold medallist and three times World Singles Champion. Indoors he has won the World title three times and the UK title in 1983. With Tony Allcock he has won countless pairs titles, including the World title in March 1987. Services to bowls brought him an MBE in 1969 and a CBE in 1980.

The idea that bowls is a game reserved for pensioners was killed off several years ago by the appearance of a number of young players in the top flight. The televising of the game, particularly at indoor venues, has clearly demonstrated that times have changed. The high level of sportsmanship remains the same as ever, but big prizes and big crowds make modern bowls as competitive and compelling as any other international sport. Having said that, I must confess to rethinking my opinion when I turned up in Clevedon for a meeting with David Bryant. For Clevedon is everything that the old bowls image would lead us to expect. It's a sleepy (actually asleep on the day I went there) seaside town with its pier hotel, its guest houses (closed for winter), tea rooms and municipal bowling rink. . .just down the prom from the crazy golf. The inhabitants seem mostly to live in old people's or convalescence homes, and the only occupation seems to be watching the seagulls overhead or looking at the half-built pier and wondering if the contractors ever will get enough money together to resume its construction.

But, of course, Clevedon has its livelier side as well as its quiet aspects. And, like Clevedon, you cannot describe bowls as simply for young or old. Perhaps that's the beauty of the game, the fact that it has remained largely unchanged while, at the same time, undergoing a revolution. When television first showed footballers hugging and kissing, every player down to the age of five did the same. When rugby at international level gets dirty, so there's a similar increase in violence right across the game. But when a bowls champion picks up a cheque for £15,000 and is suddenly being asked to enter into sponsorship deals and endorsement contracts. . .the men and women on Clevedon seafront take one more long look at the rink and send down that next wood as if nothing had ever happened. Perhaps it's not surprising that tradition tells us that Drake was playing bowls when the Spanish Armada appeared on the horizon. The players of the ancient game seem to be the most unflappable I've ever met. And the doyen of them all, David Bryant, is the perfect representative of the sport.

David has been winning championships for almost thirty years now, and he shows no sign of letting up. At the time of our meeting in wet and windy Clevedon he had just returned from winning the World Outdoor Singles title for a third time. . .at the age of fifty-six! Had I interviewed David at any time from 1958, when he won his first cap for England, until 1988 the chances are he would have just come from winning some major national or international tournament. However, David is more than just the most prolific winner of tournaments the game has ever known, he is the game's foremost ambassador and leading innovator. In other words, David Bryant is Mr Bowls. No matter what Willie Wood, Tony Allcock or the rest may achieve, it's going to be many, many years before people think of anyone other than David when thinking about the sport of bowls.

With this background in mind, I was first keen to know what kept David Bryant in Clevedon. The game of bowls had moved on, why not David?

"It's a matter of roots I suppose," explained David. "My family lived, and still live, in these parts and my club is in Clevedon too."

That seemed as good an answer as any but, as I looked out over the grey–brown waters of the Bristol Channel and felt the cold wind blow over the cliff top, I thought I'd pay my family to move rather than stay. Perhaps the family ties were very strong.

"From a bowls point of view, I owe my early interest in the game entirely to my family," David continued. "My father played regularly and also my wife's mother. In fact my father was a very useful player and he and I became indoor internationals in the same year. I've never checked to see if that's a unique sporting achievement; it's certainly one that's unlikely to be repeated in other sports."

My own father was a rugby league international and I smiled at the thought of him and me playing in the same team or gaining international honours together. I don't think my father wanted to play the "soft" sport I enjoyed, and I was certain I had no wish to get mauled and mutilated in a "game" of rugby league.

Joking aside, though, David and I shared common ground by having fathers involved in sport at the highest level. We both knew what pride they felt in seeing their sons achieve success, and we both knew what a debt we owed. Our fathers had given us encouragement in the right measure and had been there when we faced those moments of disappointment that are all part and parcel of a life in sport.

Perhaps it was inevitable that the young David Bryant should get involved in bowls, but the way in which he began is worth retelling.

"Every year," David explained, "we'd have the annual holiday in Exmouth. Two weeks, the first week on the beach and the second week watching my father compete in bowls tournaments. At first I wanted the first week to be longer and the second to be shorter. Slowly, however, I got to enjoy the bowls. One year I spotted some old lawn bowls discarded behind the greenkeeper's hut. I kept asking my father what they were and pestering him to let me play with them. In the end he got so fed up that he paid the man half-a-crown and I had my first set of woods.

"I took them home, polished them up and played non-stop. At first I used a golf ball as a jack and played on my own. But once I was good enough I gathered up some croquet balls, challenged my friends and began to get the taste for winning."

"And was it always bowls?" I asked.

41

"Far from it. In fact, I was keen on all sports. I played soccer as much as I could and was also a handy player at table-tennis and snooker. I was playing regularly in the Bristol table-tennis leagues until only five years ago and can still turn in a good frame of snooker. I think I would have liked to have played snooker professionally. . .or maybe golf.

"Anyway, it ended up as bowls, probably because of my father more than anything. He and I played many matches together in pairs and foursomes, and many against each other in the singles."

The idea of any of the Hughes clan playing serious sport against each other didn't bear thinking about. The level of competitiveness would be so high, and the level of sportsmanship so low (with E. Hughes OBE being the worst offender), that we'd never be allowed to start, let alone expected to finish. Was this the same problem with the Bryants?

"No." I didn't think it would be! Bowls isn't like that. "I can recall one incident when my father and I were playing against each other in the county championships. In those days the county championship led on to the nationals, which provided a chance for international honours. So it was an important tournament. My father and I were neck and neck, both needing a shot or two for victory. On the last end I seemed to have it in the bag when my father sent down a beauty. It stole the shot, the end and the match. As we shook hands he confessed that he had intended to miss the last shot so that I could progress to the next round; he thought I had a better chance of overall success than him. It just goes to show how well he could control his woods!"

And I never thought such cheating went on in bowls. I wonder if the controlling bodies ever heard about the incident?

That David has a love of family and home to counteract his globetrotting pursuit of bowls is clearly demonstrated by such stories – and also by the evidence of the injury he was carrying when we met.

"Fortunately I've got a short break between tournaments," he said as he tapped his injured leg, "because this really has slowed me up." I tried to imagine the sort of injury that one could sustain playing bowls; I could only assume he had dropped a wood on his toes since over-the-jack tackles don't seem to be a part of the game. So how did the injury, a pulled muscle, crop up?

"I was gardening." I might have guessed.

"I had just finished, put my slippers on and saw a damned great weed I'd missed. I turned back to get it and, with no grip on the slippers, slid down the path. I felt the muscle go."

David and I enjoyed a laugh over the incident but I did wonder if he had more trouble with maintaining fitness and avoiding injury now that he was well into his fifth decade.

"My answer is yoga. I practise it as regularly as I can, especially for my back and legs. In bowls the delivery is everything, and the delivery depends on suppleness. Yoga is ideal, you can do it any time, anywhere. It's brought me many positive benefits."

I imagined that most bowls players in Britain might be tempted to dismiss yoga as mumbo-jumbo, but it clearly needs no greater advertisement for its effectiveness than the continued success of David Bryant. And if the picture of elderly gentle folk sitting in the lotus position between woods is somehow hard to imagine, try visualising some of the contrasts within David's own character. The one that springs most immediately to mind is the way the mild-mannered and amiable David has one of the strongest wills to win I've experienced anywhere amongst my favourite British stars. Make no mistake about it, when David is playing, he's playing to win. His ability to accept defeat gracefully should not be allowed to hide the fact that he's mentally noting exactly how the victor will become the vanquished next time the two players meet.

You can tell that David enjoys winning because of the way he speaks with modest but unmistakable pride about his achievements in the game. There is not the room here to list even a part of the catalogue of success that has been the hallmark of David's career. Indoors or outdoors, in singles, pairs and fours David has rarely been without a world championship, or Olympic or Commonwealth title, since 1960.

Among all the success however, can David select a moment that really means most to him?

"Perhaps because it was the most recent, but I would nominate my 1988 World Singles title in Auckland." As he spoke, his eyes lit up at the memory. "It had all the right ingredients for me. For a start I didn't, before the tournament, hold any World title. This was the first time I'd been in this situation for many years. Second, the bowls press, such as it is, had written me off. One well-known magazine had me finishing in third place – if I was lucky! They said I was too old. And third, I played well to win and felt very satisfied with my game. I was delighted when I finally got the last shot in."

As David was speaking I noticed his smile start to fade and, as a parting comment on the world championships, he said ruefully: "I was very disappointed not to win the pairs with Tony Allcock. We reached the final which was a great game. I thought we were going to get it." Such is the competitiveness of the man.

To talk in terms of achievements on the rink is only part of the story. Apart from being the acknowledged master of playing the game, David has also led the way in developing bowls in the broadest sense. He paved the way to bowls going open in 1980, and became the first chairman of the

Players' Association. It was David who pioneered the idea of a portable rink, one that can be laid in such venues as the Albert Hall, and is now busily trying to persuade the authorities to invest in a permanent outdoor rink suitable for both spectators and television. Most of all, however, it has been David Bryant who has bridged the gap between the two ages of bowls – BT and AT, before television and after television.

David is the first to acknowledge that television has changed the game.

"Bowls only used to get an occasional mention, perhaps during a Commonwealth Games or Olympics. But televised events changed all that. So many things have followed. From a personal point of view the arrival of players like Willie and Tony and Hughie Duff have taken some of the pressure off me. I don't feel I'm expected to win every tournament. And the sight of youngsters like Nigel Smith encourage others to play too. . .not least when Nigel beat me!

"The prize money is, of course, a lot better too. But, all that aside, the most important thing is that the standard of the game has improved. The game at the very highest level is slightly better than before, but the greatest change can be seen in the 'breadth' of quality. Whereas a few years ago there were only a few players in the second tier who could beat me if I was not on top form, today there are dozens, all snapping at my heels and the heels of the other top-flight players. That's got to be good for bowls, both playing and watching."

"But has television spoiled the game in any way?" I felt impelled to ask. "I look at snooker now and wonder if it's gone too far. Are we getting bored with snooker? Could the same thing happen with bowls?"

"I don't think so, although I know what you mean. We must be careful. We don't get, and are never likely to get, quite the same exposure as either snooker or darts. And with the varieties of the game, not forgetting crown green bowls too, there's always a fresh angle for the viewers. At the moment I think we've got it about right, although I'd like to see more outdoor matches televised. I can understand the anxiety with the weather, but the game can be much more varied outdoors."

I have often wondered if televising a sport can be a mixed blessing. I know from first-hand experience the power of television. I'm very happy to say that my appearances on *A Question of Sport* and other shows have only done me good. But you can imagine the reaction I would get if I was suddenly rude or unpleasant. All those people who come up to me in hotels and restaurants to congratulate me or compliment the show would soon change their tune. It only needs a few wrong moves from sports men and women and all the good that has been done can be instantly undone.

It does seem, though, that bowls is going in the right direction. The way they congratulate each other after a good shot always amazes me. I've seen David Bryant clapping his hands politely as a championship and a £5000 first prize has just been whipped away from under his nose. I'm not sure if I could do it. Let's be honest about this, I *know* I couldn't do it. Is it a genuine response?

"Yes, but under my smiling exterior I'm thinking 'I'm going to do you next time.' The best aspect of the sportsmanlike behaviour one sees in bowls is that the young players are the most ardent practitioners of it. Some of the older chaps do get a bit grumpy at times but you can never fault the younger lads. It's actually become something of a gimmick for the sport, and if that's the result of televising the game, I'm not going to complain.

"The sport has always been good like that. Good losers abound, and bad losers can normally be cheered up with a pint afterwards. The only thing I can't stand is a bad winner. I can cope with someone being a bit quiet after losing, but there's nothing worse than somebody prattling on all night about how good they were and why they beat you."

As our chat drew to a close I realised there was one more question I wanted to put to David. But can you reasonably ask a man who has won absolutely everything in his sport what his ambitions are for the future? Wouldn't David be well within his rights to tell me that he's surely done enough and now wanted to enjoy a bit of rest. Perhaps I should ask about his plans for retirement. But one glance across the table at the fit and smiling "master" of bowls convinced me that he's probably never even given retirement a second thought. So, what does the future hold in store?

"I have one main ambition left." David's announcement came as no surprise. Bowls players everywhere take note. "That's to win a medal at the 1990 Commonwealth Games in New Zealand. My first Commonwealth Games was in 1962 when I remember David Coleman doing a piece on me. I won a medal there and have won some medals, either singles, pairs, fours or team event at every other Games I attended. There were no bowls in Jamaica in 1978 and we couldn't compete in '82 or '86 because of the rules governing open competition. But rule changes have meant that I can now enter again for 1990. I want to be there, in Auckland, and I want to win a medal. I will then be the only competitor to have won medals over five Games. At the moment Precious McKenzie, the weightlifter, and I share the record of winning at each of four Games. That's my ambition.

"After that I hope to continue playing but probably entering fewer tournaments and spending more time on my club and my business interests."

The way David so precisely defined his playing ambition suggested to me that a few bob on the result would be money well spent. He clearly knew where he was going. And as we parted I was left reflecting on the manner of the man who has done so much for bowls and so much for Britain over the past thirty years. A calm and friendly exterior hiding a fierce and steely determination. As I was about to drive away I saw David light up his famous pipe and peer into the windy distance across the Bristol Channel. I'm sure it wasn't the unfinished pier or the wheeling seagulls that occupied his mind, but a warm day and a green rink somewhere on the other side of the world.

George Best

pure genius

Undoubtedly the greatest individual player in modern British football, George Best's outstanding ball control and scoring talents made him the most exciting man in the game. He made his First Division debut at the age of seventeen years and four months in 1963, playing for Manchester United. While with United he won First Division Championship honours and a European Cup Winner's medal. He made his international debut for Northern Ireland a month short of his eighteenth birthday. In 1968 he was voted both British and European Footballer of the Year. During his career, he collected thirty-seven full caps for his country and scored nearly 150 League goals.

*I*f one of the themes of this book is a search for the magic ingredient then this could be a very short chapter indeed. The answer in George Best's case is simple, straightforward, no question about it – Georgie was born with a touch of pure genius. When they were making the deal, he was the one to draw the wild card.

And if my word is not good enough, then listen to the one man who knew more about football than any other – Bill Shankly. Liverpool were playing Manchester United in a League game at Anfield towards the end of the 1971/2 season. We needed a couple of points to win the championship while United needed everything they could to avoid the big drop (something, in fact, they didn't manage). I remember the game well; the 'Pool played well but were beaten by two goals from Bobby Charlton. The reason for the defeat was plain to see. I had been on the same park as George Best that afternoon but had not even got near him, neither had his marker nor anyone else in the Liverpool team. He had skinned us. Liverpool don't often lose at Anfield and, in those days particularly, we knew it meant the most awful bollocking from The Boss. At the end of the match we sat in the dressing room, heads down, nobody speaking. We could hear the heavy tread of Bill Shankly's feet as they came down the corridor. He had a habit of picking, first, on the more experienced players and giving them a right going-over; I must say, I fancied my chances of getting the treatment that day. So, there we sat. Shanks arrived, stood by the door and glowered at the sight of eleven heads hung in both tiredness and fright. He paused for a moment, making us all the more nervous, and then began his after-match talk. It lasted for all of eight words: "Boys," he announced, "you've just seen a genius at work." He only ever said that about two non-Liverpool players, Bestie and Tom Finney.

That match wasn't exceptional, however. It was often like that with George. He was like no one else I ever played against. And you can ask anyone who was involved in the game at that time and they will say the same. Yes, Bobby Charlton was wonderfully gifted, Jimmy Greaves was the best goal-scorer you're ever likely to see, Dennis Law had that extra bit of magic. But ask who was head and shoulders above the rest and you'll hear the same answer from everyone – the wee boy from Belfast, Georgie Best.

The question, perhaps, I ought to put to George is not "why were you so special?" but "where did it all go?", because if George was number one at football he must have also been pretty high in the league table of cocking it all up. From my own memory I can recall a couple of instances of George just not turning up for events. On one occasion in particular I remember leaving a television studio one evening following a briefing session for a World Cup programme. George was fit and well, had been sparkling in rehearsals, and was looking forward to his new job as a TV pundit. We dropped him off late, made arrangements for the car to pick him up the next morning – and didn't hear another word from him for about a fortnight!

But that was George all over. And we always forgave him for it. His friends and family, his colleagues in football and in other walks of life have all suffered from his unpredictability. The people of Belfast, his greatest and most loyal fans, have been let down time and again by their wayward son. But if you try to say one word against him you'll find yourself out of there quicker than the Pope on Orange Day.

Possibly a clue to George's character lies in the venue and time for our interview. We were to meet at Blondes, the West End wine bar and club, at 5.00 p.m. What was any self-respecting sportsman doing, at that time on a hot and sunny day, in the dark and smoky world of a London drinking spot? The answer, it later turned out, was having a cup of coffee and doing his job, namely managing the place. But I didn't actually ask the question when I was met by two of the toughest-looking characters I'll ever wish to meet. I've always thought of club bouncers as being too large and too slow to be of anything more than just deterrent value. These two were thin, fit, very Italian-looking (actually I'd say Sicilian) and looked like extras out of a Godfather movie. And they were only the waiters.

"I've come to see Georgie," I said, meekly, hoping they would ignore the times Liverpool had put one over on their favourite Italian clubs.

"Yes, come in. He won't be a minute." I was delighted to be welcomed in but not so pleased to hear the "won't be a minute" bit. In Best language, if my experience is anything to go by, that could have meant some time the following Tuesday – and it was then Wednesday. I was given a coffee and sat down to wait.

Well, they were right, Best wasn't a minute. He was three minutes, not punctual but *early* by his standards. In he strode, holding his cup of coffee, lean, smiling, healthy, looking a million pounds. The girl with him looked pretty good too; on account of her hair colour I assumed she came with the place.

"How's it going?" I asked as I got up to shake his hand.

"Pretty good, Em. Pretty good." He flashed me that famous, impish smile and in an instant I had forgiven and forgotten every missed appointment and had given myself an imaginary kick in the shin for ever thinking that the guy might have ducked the interview.

So, where do you start when you're chatting to your own personal hero? As ever, the beginning is as good a place as any. Where did it all begin?

As soon as I had asked the question a transformation occurred. They talk about Irish eyes smiling; well George's were positively shining. That dark corner of that dark London bar was lit up by his enthusiasm and his excitement. And I couldn't help but feel the same. Football, it's the greatest, and if George and I couldn't actually be out on the park playing the game, at least we could talk about it. That was clearly what he wanted.

"I can never remember a time when I wasn't playing football," he began. "I always had a ball with me. If it wasn't a proper football then I'd have a tennis ball in my pocket. All the time. I didn't want to come in during the evening; as long as my parents let me I would stay out in the street, kicking a ball about – midnight if they'd allow it. Christmas time, and all I wanted was a football."

This could have been me talking. It was a world I could understand. I wondered if George, like me, had always wanted to be a professional too.

"No, I never gave it a second thought. I just wanted to play. I never dreamed of playing professionally and certainly not of representing Northern Ireland. Football was just an everyday way of life for me. My father was keen too, although the first proper matches I watched were with my Grandad who lived fifty yards from the Glentoran Ground. I remember having a scrapbook with pictures of Glentoran at the front and, starting the other way round from the back, pictures of Wolves. It was the Wolves' heyday with their games against foreign clubs – particularly, I remember, Moscow Dynamo."

This all made sense to me. A ball in the backyard, living, eating, sleeping and, if you were lucky, dreaming about football. People say that my enthusiasm for football is catching. Well, that's a compliment, but it's not hard work being excited about something you love. And here was George Best, one of the greatest players the world has ever seen, showing just the same kind of interest and commitment. And just like one of his goal-bound dribbles, once he had started he was not going to be easily stopped.

"Although I went to Glentoran with Grandad the games I watched with my Dad were some of the most memorable. These were in the Belfast Summer League, played on what we called the 'Chicken Run'. They played almost every evening, sometimes three games in a row, so there wasn't a blade of grass to be seen. The games were total war. But there was fun too, certainly on the touchlines where somebody always had a wisecrack for every dreadful incident. In particular I remember the praise and the jokes being aimed at one man, 'Sticky' Sloane. Who he was, and what became of him, I never knew. But the name 'Sticky' Sloane has always echoed round inside my head."

52

I knew just why Georgie was so animated about his young days. It was the same for me – football, football, football. Nothing else mattered. But is it the same with kids today? It ought to be – but it's not. The worst thing is that they've got to have everything right, the kit, goals, lines marked out, before they'll even play. They don't seem to have much time for just kicking a ball about any more.

"In my young days," I told George, "you only had to give me a ball and the rest fitted into place. Twenty-one other players were conjured up out of my imagination, there were forty seconds left to play and the twin towers of Wembley were looking down at me – and this would be up against the garage doors at the back of the house. I never bothered about kit or a pitch, but I always managed to get that winning goal."

George joined in the reminiscing: "The highlight of my young days was being able to afford the magazines to stuff down my socks in place of shinpads." At this point one of the Italian brotherhood appeared bearing cups of coffee. Most welcome, as it prevented George and me going on like a couple of old men on a park bench grumbling about "the youth of today". Instead we moved on to George's Manchester United days – the times that he wore that famous red shirt being the most vivid in the memories of football fans everywhere.

The story has been told many times, but it's worth repeating, of how George turned up in Manchester following a telegram to Matt Busby from a scout. The telegram read: "I've found a genius." This was due to hard work by Bud MacFarland, who kept pushing George in his youth games in Belfast, and by the scout Bob Bishop. The result was that George, and another Belfast youngster Eric McMorley, were asked over to Manchester for a fortnight of training. Within twenty-four hours both lads were on the ferry back to Ireland. They had suffered from home-sickness and had decided to pack it in.

It was then that George's Dad took a hand in affairs, telephoned Matt Busby, and asked if his son could be given another chance. That phone call, and Matt's agreement to a second trial period, was to provide a genius with a platform for his skills and was to give Emlyn Hughes quite a few humbling moments on the football field. I'm sure that, for Best, joining United under Busby's guidance was a case of the right place at the right time, but I'm also sure that the genius in the man would have found an outlet, Manchester United or not.

So it was that Bestie went over, again, to Manchester, and there, in the company of some other great youngsters of the day such as Eamon Dunphy, Dave Sadler, Barry Fry and Barry Grayson, started his footballing career.

"At first I wasn't old enough to sign full-time professional forms so they had to find me a job. I started with being a tea boy on the Manchester Ship Canal. I didn't like it much; all I wanted to do was play football. So I stuck it for a bit until they got me another job in a sawmill. This was supposed to be more interesting. It was dreadful. I began my first morning at eight, chucked the job in at eleven, and remember going back the next day for my three hours' money!

"But I wasn't lazy. I used to train every day and not leave the ground until they kicked me out. One thing that gets me mad today is hearing professionals talk about getting stale. I couldn't get enough of it. I'd have played every day if I'd been asked. I recall when we won the Youth Cup in '63 – didn't we beat Liverpool in the semi-final [yes, thanks George] – I played in the Central League team on Saturday, first leg of the final on Monday at Swindon, Wednesday night I played for Northern Ireland against Uruguay, Thursday was the return leg of the Youth Cup at Old Trafford and, although I can't remember who against, I played again on the Saturday. I swear I would have played on Sunday if there had been a game."

The man was in full flood by now; there was no sense in even trying to attempt a tackle. "I recall my first League game was in September against West Brom. They were a good side in those days. I just couldn't wait to get out there. And it was so easy. I really found it easy. I thought, can this be the hardest league in the world? Then I was dropped for the next game and didn't get another chance until Christmas! That Christmas saw Man. U. stuffed by Burnley, I think it was on Boxing Day. I was asked to fly back from Belfast to play in the reverse fixture which was either the next day or two days later – we returned the compliment and I kept my place after that. I think it was that evening, after the Burnley match when I read my name in the Manchester 'pink 'un', that I finally thought I would make it.

"It's small incidents that I remember and that give me most pleasure." George didn't need to be asked questions any more, he was doing both parts by then! "Like the games against Ipswich." His eyes lit up at this recollection, a story about Bobby Robson. "We played them at home and I scored straight from a corner – I think it was the only goal of the match. Now think about this – I had spent something like half my adult life playing football, and a good part of that time practising kicking the ball in the goal straight from the corner flag. I always tried it at least once in a match. So you can imagine how I felt when I heard Robson, in a post-match interview, saying that Ipswich had been beaten by a fluke. 'I'll damned well show him,' is actually how I felt. So when we went to Ipswich later in the year I waited for our first corner. The rest of the team couldn't believe it. I grabbed the ball from the ref and ran over to take it myself. I lined it up and took the perfect kick. It sailed over the 'keeper, hit the inside of the far post. . .and bounced out! If that ball had gone in I would have walked over to the Ipswich bench and probably got myself booked for what I would have said."

I wondered if George Best was a member of the same club as Emlyn Hughes. I think he is. "Robson should think before he speaks," said George, in answer to my enquiry. "I've heard him after matches at Wembley praise almost every one of his team when I have known, and the press have known, and the whole crowd have known, that they have played like a bunch of wallies. It's just part of modern football. We see so much rubbish that we start calling mediocre players 'world class'."

George has got to be right about that. I know that I was good enough to captain my club and country and won almost everything there is to win in the game – but I don't expect to be labelled "world class". Today, though, you've only got to have a couple of reasonable international performances and you're up there with the greats. I asked George who, in Britain, he rated as world class since his playing days. The answer was fairly simple: "Nobody!"

"Not even Rushie and Kenny?"

'Well, Rush has scored a lot of goals in a poor league, let's see what happens in Italy. As for Kenny, well I can't see it, but that's not to say he wasn't the best of his generation."

"So, has football got worse?"

"I think so – but that's always going to be open to argument. And, anyway, I'm biased. But what I do know is that football is less fun today. And I will argue with anybody on that one."

Well I wouldn't argue with Bestie on that. I've never known a more serious bunch than some of today's professional footballers and managers. In my day it was bloody hard work, but you had a laugh too. I wondered whom George remembered in particular. As I asked this question I knew whom I was thinking of.

"Joe Mercer," says George. Got it in one. "He was one of many, but I do recall he loved his game and loved a laugh. Up in Manchester there are as many stories about him as there are about Shanks in Liverpool. I remember him telling me about you, Emlyn." Here we go. "Apparently, later in your career you had slowed down a bit – but you were still as hard. On one occasion you hacked a winger down when he had got past you. The referee ran over and started remonstrating with you. 'That was a bad foul, Hughes. That was a very late tackle.' You replied: 'Late tackle? But I got here as quickly as I could!'"

Thanks for that George. Very funny. In fact I can't remember Joe talking about Bestie but I often think of the happy times the England squad had when Mercer was caretaker manager. Once we were training and Joe was talking to me about team selection. We were watching one particular First Division full-back. I didn't think much of him. Although he was a hard worker he was not a team man, and, in fact, always seemed a little surly. Joe asked mem what I thought. I hesitated, so Joe said: "Come on, Emlyn, be honest. He's a miserable so-and-so. We're not having him in the team." That summed up Joe's approach.

Who else did George remember?

"Rodney Marsh. When Rodney and I came back from America and went to Fulham we were thought of as the odd couple because we were always laughing. There were many others too, not big names but just good footballers who played hard, but enjoyed a laugh. Last year I was on holiday in Spain when I heard a familiar voice behind me saying: 'Turn round George. Let's have a look at you.' It was Graham Williams, a Welsh international from West Brom with whom I had many duels. He stood there for a moment, looking at me, then said: 'That's better. Do you know, I'd only ever seen your arse before!'"

Was everything better back then? I'm beginning to believe it myself. Did George and I play in the golden age of football? Well, not really. For a start there was Don Revie's Leeds United. The worst thing that ever happened to British football in my opinion. What did George think?

"I hated going over there to play. In fact most of their team could really play a bit – but their attitude and approach were all wrong. Stop you playing first. We've seen those famous couple of games when they really turned it on. They did that because they were six or seven goals to the good and weren't afraid of losing.

"Revie did a lot of harm. He was typical of the managers – and there's a lot of them around today – who praise their players for their work rate. That shouldn't be an extra; that's a basic requirement. I always prided myself on fitness and was probably as pleased as at any time when Matt Busby said I was one of the best tacklers for the ball he had seen. When I lost it I wanted it back, and I was prepared to chase a man right across the park to get it.

"Look at our European Cup Final triumph in 1968. We were fit enough to storm it in extra time." George thought for a moment, perhaps remembering the same heart-stopping moment as I was.

"What about that last-minute save by Stepney from Eusebio?" I asked him.

"At the time it didn't frighten me too much because Alex had it covered and I knew, we all knew, that Eusebio would blast it. Had it been Greavsie we would have been dead. But that save gave us extra time and our fitness, team work and a sense of destiny gave us the match. Mind you, I think it did a lot of harm too. After that the Club seemed to relax. We had won the European Cup so what was left? I could sense the anti-climax. United haven't won the League for twenty years and I was the last player to score more than twenty league goals in a season. That's disgraceful. It's a crime too, especially when I see some of the players who pull on the red shirt today."

George looked rather sad, almost wistful. The spell of the past had him gripped. If I didn't ask him then, I never would.

"George. You say that's a crime. I think what you did was a crime, too. You should have given us five more years of football. Why did you leave the game when you did?"

"I was hooked on a drug. Something just took over. I can't explain it, I can only look at other people who seemingly had everything and see how they threw it all away. Elvis, Hendrix, and not so long ago the Irish lad, Phil Lynott."

George stared at his empty coffee cup. How often, I thought, had that been an empty whisky glass.

"I spoke to my son a while back and told him I was coming over to see him. Do you know, he said that I shouldn't promise anything because I'd only let him down. I should just turn up and surprise him. When your own son says that, you know things are bad. And situations like that knock me back into shape. But then I'll have a drink – and with me I can't just have one drink – and I'll be off for two or three days and at the end I won't remember where I've been and whom I've been with. I once went thirty-two days without eating. Things like that frighten you. But I can't help it.

"I lost six weeks once. Couldn't remember a thing. Alcohol changes people. It changes their moods. And I'm a victim."

The honesty of the man was chilling. He was sitting there, looking fit and well, he was in training for a series of charity matches, running a successful business and saying that tomorrow, or maybe the next day, perhaps after just one half of lager, he could piss it all away. But his eyes tell you it's the truth, and your head tells you the same. It's your heart that wishes it wasn't so.

We were both sitting there, in silence, as the first customer of the evening came in. A waiter walked over to the door and on went the lights. The spell was broken. As our table was being cleared I sensed that all those wonderful memories were being cleared away with the cups – for the moment at least.

We rose to part and I realised that the easiest thing in the world, perhaps the most obvious thing in the world right then, would be to offer George a drink. "Let me buy you a drink?" or "How about one for the road?" Six-word sentences that might just as well be saying "Here, let me screw you up." And the sad thing is I think George might even have accepted. Is it his fault that he's always too eager to please, wouldn't want to disappoint an old pal? I'm a footballer, not a psychiatrist. So I leave the diagnosis to the pros.

As I left, George gave me another of his wonderful Irish smiles – even the famous dark beard couldn't hide the fact that his whole face was smiling. In an instant I'd happily forgotten all about Georgie's problem and had been transported back to Anfield. I've just, for once in my life, got the ball off George and have pushed it a few yards in front of me. As I start my run I find my shirt pulled tightly from behind – held by George. The ball runs out of play for a United throw. The ref doesn't see (do they ever?), and as I go over to tell George exactly what I think of him he flashes me that same smile. Do you know, in that moment, I think I forgave him.

Sean Kerly

playing just for fun

Great Britain's hockey striker Sean Kerly has earned a reputation as great as any of this country's top football players. In the Asian hockey-playing nations he is hailed as a superstar. The twenty-eight-year-old Southgate amateur was a member of the Great Britain side which won the bronze medal in the 1984 Olympics and a member of the England team which reached the final of the World Cup in 1986, only to lose 2–1 to Australia. Born in 1960 in Herne Bay, he works as a merchandising manager with a high-street jewellers.

*B*efore approaching any of the interviews for this book I did my homework, checked up on a few facts and figures about the person I was going to talk to and gave some thought to the types of question I was going to ask. When coming to meet Sean Kerly, the man who has spearheaded both England's and Britain's hockey attack for the last few seasons and one of the men who has become a symbol of the rebirth of the old game, I found I was focusing on only one point. That was the fact that Sean Kerly was, and is, an amateur sportsman. Of course, there are millions of people in Britain who play just for the fun of it – but not many are competing at the same international level as Sean. Because of the recent successes of the English and British teams, hockey has found itself under the media spotlight. The players, particularly Sean and his goalkeeper colleague Ian Taylor, have been given the full treatment. Television appearances, guest speaking assignments and even being recognised in the street are all features of their new lives.

For Sean it must have been a major change. Suddenly he's involved in a world which is normally the preserve of the professional and which usually brings financial rewards to compensate for the extra effort and pressure. And yet Sean, as hockey player and true Olympian, remains strictly an amateur.

Apart from wondering about the problem of being an amateur in a world dominated by money, I suppose I also had certain ideas about what it means to be playing because you want to and not because you are paid to. What about one's attitude to criticism? How do players cope with training if it isn't compulsory? Are winning and losing as important to the amateur as they are to the professional? And I also wondered about how people like Sean feel when they know they can't earn a penny and yet see other sports stars getting plenty and doing a lot less.

The more I thought about my question the more I realised I was looking at myself and my own approach to sport. How would I have coped? Would Emlyn Hughes have been able to put as much into playing football as he did if he had not been paid for it from the day he left school? Would I have come as far as Sean if my chosen sport had been hockey and not football?

"The fact is," said Sean in response to my first question about the origins of his ability, "I would never had played hockey if we hadn't moved for my father's work. We were living in Macclesfield and I was football mad. You know the sort of thing. All I wanted to do was play or watch football. Occasionally we'd go to see United; that was in the days of Bestie of course and there was a special feel about Old Trafford. Then one day we just upped sticks and moved to Herne Bay in Kent. I was sent to school in Ramsgate, a school where they played rugby and hockey.

"I was pretty fed up about missing the football, but sport was sport and

I threw myself into whatever was going. I was too small for rugby but got on quite well with hockey.

"There was one other reason for preferring hockey and that was the master in charge, a bloke called 'Tommy' Thomas." As soon as Sean mentioned the name of a respected teacher from his early days I realised that I was on familiar ground. So many top achievers in sport owe a debt to a teacher or a coach. Without the Tommy Thomases of this world many a spark would have remained unignited, many a potential not realised.

"What was there special about this teacher?" I asked.

"He made us laugh. He was probably very good at coaching hockey and he was certainly extremely enthusiastic too. But the main reason we all liked him at school was that we enjoyed his lessons and had fun playing in his teams. When I started to improve at the game and got county trials and had to travel around a bit, Tommy was always there with the car. He and my father both put in their share of the miles to get me to important games in those days. Tommy is still as enthusiastic as ever; I saw him just a couple of weeks ago at a match."

I briefly tried to remember my hockey teacher, a fairly pointless exercise because my school didn't have such a thing. In fact, I don't remember seeing any of the schools in Barrow with a hockey pitch. There was football and rugby league. Hockey was for toffs. Being out of touch a little, I asked Sean if this was still the picture.

"Very much so. Public schools and grammar schools, where they still exist, are the places for hockey. Many comprehensives play hockey, but many more don't. Whether it's just the image the game has or whether it's directly related to the school situation I don't know, but my colleagues are lawyers, teachers, solicitors and so on. I haven't come across many brickies or chippies in the years I've spent playing the game."

"But the recent television coverage will probably change all that," I suggested.

"No, I don't think so. At least I haven't seen any evidence of it so far. If you think about it, it's very hard to just walk into a club and join. You tend to go along with a friend or colleague. Since most of the players are professional people anyway, they are likely to bring along similar people. There has to be a major change at the school level before things really get moving. I'd like to see it, but I'm not very optimistic."

"Perhaps winning an Olympic gold medal will help?"

"It may do. We'll see when we win it!"

In our conversation up till then I had sensed, in Sean, both a sense of loyalty and dedication to the game and yet, at the same time, a feeling of disappointment or resignation about it. Perhaps I was mistaken and he just didn't like the meal we were eating. I decided to ask anyway.

"No, the meal is fine, thanks." So what about hockey?

"I have to say that our recent achievements have been in spite of the governing bodies and not because of them. To my mind they have not recognised the great potential of the game, they have not built on the successes of recent months and years and they are not really in tune with what is going on. Having said that, the administrators are mostly amateur and perhaps I shouldn't expect too much. But in this country the standard of play is among the highest in the world. We really should capitalise on this and make the most of our newly found international status."

I've heard so many Brits go over the top in praising and promoting their own sport and the players in it that I always remain a bit dubious. For example, how many times have we heard that a footballer is "world class", only to see him fail time and again in big matches? How often have the armchair public been led to believe that a world heavyweight champion or a future Wimbledon winner is, at last, amongst us? So is Sean Kerly's assessment another example of wishful thinking? Are we really that good?

"Yes. In the World Cup England were, I'm sure, the second-best team on parade. We didn't fear anybody although I don't think we were as good as Australia. When it comes to the Olympics, and we play as Britain, we can be as good as any other team in the competition."

I reminded Sean that this book will be appearing around the time of the 1988 Olympics and that he may be asked to account for his optimism. He didn't seem to be too worried. I also asked Sean to remind me why he sometimes plays for England and sometimes for Great Britain.

"In normal internationals, and in the World Cup, the home countries are allowed to enter separately. In the Olympics, however, we enter as Great Britain because that is how we are affiliated to the International Olympic Movement. We shouldn't forget that our bronze medal at the 1984 Los Angeles Olympics only came about because of the oddities of the system.

"Because Great Britain doesn't play as a team between Olympics we have no record of achievement to enable our international standing to be assessed. So, we weren't invited to the 1984 Games. About six weeks before, however, the Soviet Union pulled out for political reasons and we were asked to act as a substitute. It seems ironic that our great success there, and the subsequent burst of interest in hockey in the UK, was indirectly due to the American invasion of Grenada."

Looking back to those Olympics there were, of course, many great moments to savour. But for the truly patriotic, and they don't come more patriotic than me, some of the most exciting and moving scenes were reserved for the hockey pitch. Not only were there the unbridled and spontaneous victory celebrations to enjoy, but there were also these strange tales of sportsmen having fun. At a Games where the seriousness of competition was often allowed to dominate the fact that amateur sport is supposed to be about taking part, the British Olympic hockey side were a shining example of how to mix achievement with enjoyment, skill with a bit of skylarking.

"I know there was some criticism of us in the Olympic Village, but I think we got things in perspective. We had only had six or seven weeks' notice of our participation so it wasn't like the culmination of a lifetime's ambition. Clearly, for some athletes, the Games represented the very pinnacle of their lives. I wouldn't ever like to place so much emphasis on one sporting competition, even if it is the Olympic Games. For the British hockey team it was just great to be there, mixing with people who had only ever been names in newspapers or faces on the television to us in the past. We trained hard but, each evening, we'd sit on one of the balconies in the village and laugh and joke. I can't remember any of us drinking – I certainly only had one beer the entire time I was in America – but sometimes, I expect, we got a bit noisy. So what. We didn't do any harm and our attitude paid dividends on the pitch."

As Sean spoke I sensed that the Olympics actually meant a good deal more to him than he was making out. I challenged him about this; were the Olympics special to him?

"Our first match was against Kenya," Sean explained. "The whistle went for the start and I found my eyes were actually getting moist. Sean Kerly was an Olympian. No matter what else happened in my life, I had competed in an Olympic Games. I'm quite serious when I tell you that I had tears on my face for the first few minutes of the match." I could tell he was being quite serious.

"Fortunately for me, and for the team," he continued, "I scored after ten minutes and so got into my stride fairly early on in the tournament. Scoring that goal also helped me see each match as another international and forget, for a time at least, how I felt inside."

Pride in playing for one's country, especially at such a big event as the Olympic Games, is something that I think is excusable. In my case, and I'm sure it was the same for Sean, the pride is mixed with humility. You know you're there because of your ability. You can also take pleasure from the fact that wearing your country's colours is a reward for all the sacrifices and hard work you've had to endure to get there. But you also know that many other people have worked equally hard but they've just lacked that bit of skill, that touch of class and, most importantly, that little piece of luck. You owe it to them, as much as to yourself, to do your very best.

The day I first pulled on an England jersey was possibly the most special of all the great days I enjoyed in my career. The match against the Dutch in Holland was not especially memorable, but the feeling of pride and satisfaction will live with me forever. Was it the same for Sean?

"My first international shirt was on – and off – within ten minutes!" Sean answered with a smile.

"My debut was against the Polish national side on a rainy, cold March day. The match was at Crystal Palace and there must have been at least fifty people in the ground. I do recall trying to savour the moment when I actually put on an England shirt for the first time although I was very nervous at the time and more worried about my performance than the significance of my appearance. Anyway, we got kitted up, trotted out onto the park, and discovered the Poles were wearing the same colours as us. Hence my shirt was back on the dressing-room floor inside ten minutes. We found some alternative kit but, as you can imagine, the whole thing was a bit of an anticlimax."

Sean's first appearance for England was eight years ago. I wondered if things had changed since then.

"I can honestly say, media coverage and public interest notwithstanding, a player making his debut tomorrow could face just the same level of organisation. We haven't really come on a great deal although, as you know, the World Cup did bring in some quite large crowds."

"So, if your international career didn't start all too well, what would you say was the best moment of your life so far?" I asked.

"Probably," Sean thought for a moment, "my first woman." I suppose I asked for that response. I was tempted to ask him to tell me about it but I decided that it was probably best to stick to hockey.

From the outside it seems that the 1984 Olympics and the 1987 World Cup have changed the face of hockey in Britain. But from what Sean had said, the changes appear to be only skin deep. Is this a true assessment of the situation?

"Pretty much so," was Sean's carefully considered view of my suggestion. "As I said earlier, the organisation is still dominated by amateurs and that will always create problems. But, alongside the essentially shambolic way things occur, we're getting some of the trappings of more intensely professional sports. Take, for example, our training. Now I've always managed to keep myself fit. I know what I need to do and I have never let myself play in an international if I didn't think I was one hundred per cent ready. Suddenly, for the Olympics and also since then, we're expected to knuckle down to five-mile runs, shuttles, running up hills etc.

"Now, I don't mind making the effort if it's going to help me, but some of the training was simply tiring me out and getting us, as a team, nowhere. It's no bloody good going out there super fit if you can't actually play the game."

I understood exactly what was angering Sean. He would have liked Bill Shankly's approach. When we were playing in several competitions he would be content to allow the matches to be the physical training. We'd work on tactics and skills, of course, but we'd get fit for matches by playing matches. As for running up hills? "When they build a hill in the middle of a football pitch, that's when we start running up and down them," was Shanks' approach. Apart from this, I think Bill respected his players too much to be too strict with them. It was a fine balance, keeping them under control but allowing them to determine, pretty much, how they wanted to act. It worked with Bill, though, and I think it can work with any group of dedicated professionals. . .but there I go again, thinking in terms of professional sport. If you're an amateur and don't like something, what do you do?

"Tell them to get lost." Sean had no doubts about this. "I play for fun and when somebody starts taking the fun out of it, then I'm off."

"Even if it meant losing your place in the international squad?" I thought I would test Sean's resolve on this point.

"I don't like to think about it in those terms. Happily it hasn't come to that yet." The answer was very diplomatic. "But I must put international hockey into perspective. I play in internationals because I'm successful with my club side, Southgate. I'm a club man first; the rest is a bonus. It's at Southgate that I have my fun, enjoy a good social life and find what I need in my life apart from my work – and the relationship with my girlfriend. I could live without hockey if I ceased to enjoy it; I just can't see that day around the corner."

"And is it enjoyment that keeps you at it?" I asked this, beginning to feel that I was, at last, uncovering the true amateur. Sean's answer was as "professional" as any I can remember.

"What really drives me on is burning desire to prove that I'm not only as good as the next man, but I'm better. I want to win a gold medal at the Olympics with Britain and a World Cup winner's medal with England. I want to be known around the world, wherever hockey is played. When I know I'm the best, then I'll enjoy every moment of it.

"If you ask any of my team colleagues, at either club or international level, they'll tell you that they enjoy hockey. But what they really mean is they enjoy winning at hockey. It's the desire to win that keeps us playing as hard as we can. Then, when we win, we all enjoy it."

Elsewhere in this book I've spoken about John Francome as being the professional amateur. He got paid for doing what he enjoyed. I might be tempted to tag Sean as the amateur professional. He doesn't get paid but shares much the same attitude to his sport as many a professional. The more we talked the more I liked the personable young man sitting opposite me, and the less I relished the thought of ever meeting him on a sports field. Happily we don't compete in the same area, but I wouldn't like to be facing up to him. I have this feeling that he might search me out in the first few minutes, just to test my determination. He confessed to having been banned from playing cards at home because he makes such a fuss when he loses; just the sort of player to have on your team and not against you.

The business of amateur and professional is something from which there is no escape. One of the last questions I put to Sean concerned his immediate ambitions. Was there anything going to happen to him for which he would like to be remembered? His answer to this was not to repeat his desire to reach the very top at hockey. No, top of Sean's current list of ambitions was to win the approval of the jewellery company for whom he had just begun working.

"I was a transport manager but recently became a merchandising manager, working in jewellery. It's a good job, with good prospects. At the moment, being fairly new, I'm still finding it a bit strange and bit of a struggle."

I found it hard to comprehend how he could put this top of his list of priorities, but realised how seriously he obviously took his work when he told me that the switch of jobs had cost him quite a bit of holiday.

"The new company grants me six weeks holiday a year, which is fair, and I have to fit in my hockey around that."

I tried to imagine how some of the football managers I knew would react to their players being unavailable for matches because they were working. I shudder to think what Shanks would have made of it.

And, on the subject of work, Sean had to dash off from our appointment because we were meeting in his lunch hour. A different world from the one I knew as a sportsman. And very different again from the world of the average sports fan. Most people play their sports for fun, never think of getting paid and generally enjoy whatever it is they're doing. A very few actually get paid a living wage for playing their sport. And then there are the Sean Kerlys. All the pressure and none of the cash; all the expectation but not much support. But I suppose we wouldn't be true Brits if we didn't go about these things in a typically muddled and amateurish way. And Sean, he's not really the complaining type. He'll just go on doing his best until, one day, he will decide to quit. All we know is that whatever he does at the moment is inspired by true motivation; nobody can accuse him of doing anything "just for the money".

HRH The Princess Royal

against all the odds

The Princess Royal, who began riding as a three-year-old, has probably done more than any other individual to put the sport of eventing on the map. At her first Badminton in 1971, she achieved a creditable fifth place on Doublet. In the same season, she won the individual gold medal in the European Championships. Other career highlights include being part of the 1976 Olympic team in Montreal with her horse Goodwill. More recently, she has ridden winners in both National Hunt racing and flat racing. The Princess's level of commitment to her sport is demonstrated by her support for the Riding for the Disabled Association, of which she is President.

I felt like pinching myself just to check that it was all actually happening. Was it really Emlyn Hughes, the boy from 94 Blake Street, Barrow-in-Furness, sitting there at the table? Well, it certainly seemed real enough. Barbara, my wife, was sitting next to me, and across the table were my children, Emma and Emlyn. But surely that couldn't be Her Royal Highness The Princess Royal, pouring out the tea and offering round the sandwiches? What was I doing there, at Gatcombe Park, in the company of Princess Anne and her family as guest for the weekend? How had my ability to kick a ball about led to this, a most memorable and enjoyable event?

For the answer to that question we need to go back to the end of the 1974 FA Cup Final. Liverpool had beaten Newcastle United 3–0 that day and I proudly led the team up the famous thirty-nine steps to collect the trophy. Guest of honour that day, and presenting the Cup and medals, was Her Royal Highness, Princess Anne. We shook hands, she congratulated me and the team, and then I, as is the nature of the occasion, got caught up in the kind of celebrations for which the Liverpool fans are famous. But I didn't forget the moment. I knew just how pleased my father was for me to have met a member of the Royal Family. And I was pretty chuffed too; for a self-confessed patriot and royalist it was quite a thrill to receive the Cup from Princess Anne.

A couple of years passed before I had the opportunity to meet her again. I was at Anfield for the 1976 Grand National and Anne and her husband, Captain Mark Phillips, were assisting David Coleman on a feature for BBC television. I persuaded David Coleman to introduce me to Mark Phillips who, in turn, presented me to his wife. Our first exchange was unforgettable.

I said, "It's a great honour to meet you. Actually we met once before at the 1974 FA Cup Final, but I don't suppose you remember me."

"That's funny," she said, smiling, "I was thinking that you wouldn't remember me!"

That established me as the leader of her fan club, although I know that my position would be challenged by a number of other people from the world of sport. Our paths crossed from time to time, and I was always impressed by both her friendly charm and sharp wit. However, the chain of events that led to the invitation to visit Gatcombe, and the privilege of being able to interview her for this book, began back in 1986.

I have to confess now that Barbara and I were having a row. In true married-couple style it was about nothing but, nevertheless, there we were – not speaking to each other. The 'phone rang and both Barbara and I stared at each other. I looked away as if to say "you pick it up". Barbara carried on ironing. The 'phone carried on ringing. Eventually I called out.

"Answer that will you."

"You answer it. It'll be for you," came the fond reply.

The 'phone kept on ringing. We glowered at each other until, just to shut the thing up, I picked the phone up.

"Hello," I rasped down the mouthpiece.

"Is that Emlyn Hughes?" came the polite and mannered response.

"Yes."

"Hello Emlyn. This is Mark Phillips here."

"Yes." I always did have a way with words.

"I'm calling about a forthcoming event I'm organising." As I heard this I put my hand over the mouthpiece and called over to Barbara.

"Ever heard of a Mark Phillips? He wants me for some do or other."

"No. Ask him what company he's from," Barbara answered.

"Excuse me Mr Phillips, but where are you calling from?"

"From Gatcombe Park."

Now, I've been called slow on the football field, but normally I'm pretty quick off it. But on this occasion I must have been half asleep. . .no, fully asleep. For, instead of standing to attention and starting my apologies for being so abrupt, I put my hand over the mouthpiece again and said to Barbara: "He says he's from Gatcombe Park."

The look on Barbara's face said it all. I had visions of being asked to hand back my OBE. "Help" was all I could think. Still I managed to get through the rest of the conversation without making too much of a fool of myself – Barbara listened in on the extension 'phone and said I sounded a little startled but otherwise OK – and found I had been invited to spend the Saturday at the three-day event at Gatcombe which was organised by Captain Mark Phillips. I was honoured and delighted and happily accepted the offer.

It was at this showpiece equestrian event that I met Her Royal Highness again. In the course of our conversation she said to me, quite out of the blue: "Do bear me in mind if ever you get a spare place on your team for *A Question of Sport*."

"Of course," I mumbled my reply, hardly taking in what she had suggested.

I spent the rest of the day trying to steal a private word with Mark Phillips, "The Captain" as everyone, including his wife, at Gatcombe seemed to call him. When I did get him alone I put the question to him: "Do you think Anne is serious when she says she wants to be on *A Question of Sport*?"

"Did she ask you?" The Captain put the ball back in my court.

"Yes, sort of."

"Well, then I'm sure she's serious. She never misses a programme, and she always records them on the video when she's away. We have to sit and watch while she calls out the right answers."

I drove back home that night nursing this amazing possibility. What a show that would be, with Princess Anne in my team. Live that one down, Bill Beaumont. But there was a lot of discussion to take place first. Would the BBC think it appropriate; would the Royal Household have reasons for vetoing the plan; and would I have a spare place in my team? Would I heck, she only had to name the date.

Eventually we got it all fixed up and the programme went out, not only with some of the highest rating figures ever achieved by the Beeb, but with some of the best moments ever witnessed by viewers of the series.

A happy relationship was established and I was delighted that Princess Anne not only agreed to the interview for the book but kindly invited me and my family to spend the Saturday night of the Gatcombe eventing weekend with her family at her home. So that, in a nutshell, is how Crazy Horse ended up taking tea with members of the Royal Family on a hot Saturday in August.

But before I can go on, I should just point out that it wasn't any hot Saturday in August. It was the first weekend of the 1987 football season and, between mouthfuls of tea, I managed to catch the news from "Smithy", one of Princess Anne's security guards, that Liverpool had beaten Arsenal 2–1 at Highbury. Enough to bring a smile to my face – hoping that the Gatcombe household aren't Arsenal supporters of course! Surely not, they seem much too sensible for that.

The Gatcombe event, as I have been describing it, is the Croft Original British Open Horse Trials Championship, a very important milestone in the three-day eventing calendar and a crucial test for those riders and horses that are hoping to make the British team for the European Championships. And watching it that weekend I was reminded of just what a demanding sport three-day eventing is.

The first category of the competition is the dressage where horse and rider have about seven or eight minutes to complete a sequence of clearly defined movements within a strictly confined area. These movements include such things as walking, trotting and cantering the horse in tight circles, along straight lines and in a sequence of zig-zags across the arena. One manoeuvre that I enjoyed looking out for was keeping the horse absolutely still for five seconds – this is particularly hard when you've got a horse that has been trained for an arduous four-kilometre cross-country course, has just been warmed up with some preliminary moves and is then asked to stand stock still. I think, however, if I had a go at the dressage I would have great difficulty in getting the moves in the right order. The rules point out that the dressage must be done strictly from memory.

The dressage takes place in the main arena, as does the second part of the competition, the show jumping. This is a very tense time for the competitors. As they are only half way through the whole event they are never sure whether to try for a careful, and hopefully clear, round or whether to go all out for a quick time and put the pressure on their rivals when it comes to the cross-country section. Watching the dressage I can sometimes imagine myself taking part, but when it comes to the show jumping I'm reminded that I'm a coward where horses are concerned (riding, that is – I wish I was more of a coward where betting was concerned) and decide to content myself with remaining a spectator.

Perhaps the most exciting, and, at Gatcombe, the most scenic part of the competition is the cross-country course. The twenty-nine fences are spread around the eighty-two acres of the Park. The surroundings are so pretty and the competitors are seemingly so relaxed and confident that one can forget that this trial will mark the end of international aspirations for some riders and horses and possibly the start of the road to gold medals for others. The end of the cross-country marks the end of the competition. The points awarded for each of the three events are totalled and an order of merit is established. Coupled with the congratulations at the end of this event is the knowledge that another prize is on offer, a place in the British eventing team.

It's interesting to note that selection for the British team is on a rider and horse partnership. The pair are selected, not just the rider. For this reason some riders are actually going through the whole competition twice – on different horses. British stars such as Virginia Leng, Lucinda Green and Jane Thewall and New Zealander Mark Todd took this option.

Britain's most famous horsewoman, HRH the Princess Royal, was not taking part but her husband, Captain Mark Phillips, was. He was particularly anxious to impress the selectors, being in contention for one of those prized team places. However, because he designed the cross-country course, and because he was "playing at home", the competition rules only allowed him to compete *hors concours*, namely on his own and outside the main event.

This was one of the first things I raised with Her Royal Highness when we met.

"I think it's particularly hard on The Captain," she responded. "For a start it's harder to ride on your course anyway because the horse, and possibly the rider, doesn't get that special sense of occasion that's necessary to bring out the best in one. And to ride out of the main competition only increases the problem. We'll see what happens."

As she spoke she looked out towards the course. Perhaps she would like to be competing this year?

"No thank you. I'm happy now just to ride for pleasure and to fit in, whenever I can, the occasional race for David Nicholson."

We could clearly have begun a long conversation then about racing – something people keep telling me I know nothing about – but I wanted to find out a little about the beginnings of The Princess Royal's riding career first. And, even before that, I had a most pleasant duty to perform.

"First, Ma'am, may I wish you a very happy birthday."

"Thank you." I sensed I was being urged not to dwell on the point. Change the subject, Emlyn.

"Where I would like to start is at the beginning." Very astute Emlyn, get on with it. "When did you first learn to ride?"

"That's almost like asking me when I first learned to walk. I honestly cannot remember a time when I couldn't ride. Of course I was fortunate in having a mother who was happy to encourage me, and I also had plenty of room to practise. So I've been riding for as long as I can remember. But I didn't get involved in competitions or the kind of Pony Club activities that one normally associates with young children." I wondered if this was one of the disadvantages that I believe have stood in the way of Her Royal Highness. Was she, because of her position, prevented from joining a club and discouraged from competing?

"No, not at all. The reason was that we rarely had two holidays in the same place so I was never settled into a routine. There wasn't an obvious local club for me. I would ride at Sandringham or Windsor and at school."

"And did you have a riding teacher?"

"No, not really. Sybil Smith is often quoted as having taught me to ride but that's simply not true. In fact some of the tuition I received made me seriously cross. It seemed to take some of the fun away from it and be leading nowhere. I was very close to giving up riding at the age of about sixteen or seventeen. I suppose I still enjoyed it but it didn't seem to be getting anywhere. If somebody had said I couldn't ride again at that stage I wouldn't have been too bothered.

"Then I was introduced to Alison Oliver and everything changed. I started competing, and within two and a half years was at Badminton. Because of my late start in eventing I went straight into adult competition. I think this helped me because I was less nervous than some competitors. For example, Mark had been, since he was a child, going to the big events and looking forward to the day when he would be there as a competitor. He would walk the course thinking: 'Some day, it will be my turn.' I never dreamed that I would get involved in competing and so didn't have that build-up of expectation and nerves.

"I suppose, looking back, I didn't know enough about it to be really nervous. It might be different now that I know all the things that can go wrong."

Whatever the reason for her early aptitude, Princess Anne, as she was then titled, soon made her name in the sport. She won the individual gold medal at the European Championships held at Burleigh in 1971 and followed that success, four years later, with individual and team silver medals at Luhmuhlen, Germany, in the same competition. This period of sustained achievement culminated in selection for the British team for the three-day event at the Montreal Olympics in 1976. I recall seeing her at an interview before the Olympics when she looked far from easy. In fact, she looked a little like the rather blunt and aggressive lady that sections of the press used to make her out to be. How does she remember those days?

"It was only to be expected, but I seemed to be the only member of the team that the press wanted to interview. Many of my answers probably were rather short, trying to get them passed on to others in the squad. They were all marvellous but they may have felt a little miffed at one member of the team getting all the attention. Also, inevitably, there were some silly questions that were constantly repeated. 'Were we going to win the gold?' was one I recall that was asked time and again. How should I know?"

This mention of the press gave me the opening I wanted. The relationship between the Royal Family and the press is one of the most bizarre aspects of the way we Brits behave. I don't need to go into detail about the way the press have treated the Royal Family. What is without doubt is that the coverage has been pretty enormous in recent years and some of it has been absurdly intrusive. I know just how difficult it can be with the press keen to hear, and probably misquote, everything you say. How much worse must it have been for Her Royal Highness. I hope my question didn't fall into the category of "silly" but I was keen to know just how she felt about it.

"When I'm competing it's part of my private life and not my public one – so I reckon the press are fair game, especially if they choose to get in the way. And of course I don't get the sporting press covering the events; it's normally the Royal Family watchers. However, I have noticed a change in recent years, mostly after my trip to Africa for Save the Children. The journalists and television crews who came on that venture reported the whole thing very responsibly. Subsequently I have been treated a lot better. Let's face it, before then I was often pictured as a second cousin to a horse; today my sporting interests are reported much more in context. For once in my life I wish I could give them something more to write about – a few more winners for example."

"But you do have a reputation for being, perhaps, a little undiplomatic at times." Perhaps I was being a little undiplomatic, although I was sure that Her Royal Highness would understand what I was getting at. "Is this a fair comment Ma'am?"

"Things I say under my breath often get reported as if I had come out in the open and said them. It does irritate me but there's not a lot I can do about it. You would say things under your breath if, every time you made a mistake while competing, hundreds of cameras flashed and pens started scribbling." Me? I wouldn't have the self-control to keep the comments down. I would be out there shouting and cursing at everyone in sight. Putting myself in her position, with all the pressures of being a member of the Royal Family, makes me realise just how hard her sporting life must have been. Far from being in a privileged position and finding everything laid on a plate, was it more difficult for Her Royal Highness to achieve exactly what she did?

"Not harder – but every bit as hard. Perhaps I didn't have some of the worries of other competitors, but then I did have some extra pressures as you've just pointed out. Actually being a member of the Royal Family is not all it's cracked up to be. I sometimes compare my daily life as like living in a hotel – but with poorer service. Of course I get advantages but some people think it's all like *Dallas*. That's absolute piffle!" Just moments before The Princess Royal said this she had being making the tea for the host of helpers at the house, organising her children with their scones and sandwiches and personally passing round large slices of her birthday cake – not the kind of performance we associate with Sue Ellen.

"But what about the rest of the Family, Ma'am. What was their attitude to your decision to compete at such a high level?"

"Surprise. There was not really a precedent for what I did. But there was no opposition." Who would have dared, I thought.

As I looked at my notes I realised that I'd been drawn into the trap of talking about Her Royal Highness as a member of the Royal Family and not as a champion sportswoman. I have always maintained, with anyone that will listen to me, that The Princess Royal is a little bit special. This was true when she was competing and it's true now in her public life. The determination and effort that went into winning medals is visible today in the work she puts in for the numerous charities with which she is associated. And anyone who has worked with her will tell you the same, she's a different class. Perhaps, as the unofficial leader of the fan club, I ought to tell her. Especially I ought to tell her how much her sense of humour is appreciated. But I don't think calling her "different class" is the best approach.

"Ma'am," I began, "you are. . ." I've started so I'll finish. But what should I say?

"Yes." You're keeping Her Royal Highness waiting, Emlyn.

"You are. . ." In eventing terms I was poised on the highest part of the water jump. The Princess Royal looked at me. "You are a cracker." Can Emlyn Hughes just have said that? Oh, no. I've started to fall towards the water. Can I save myself?

"What I mean," I'm struggling to retain my balance, "is that you are good for a laugh." Splash! Even as I began to search for something else to say the headline writers were sharpening their pencils: "Ex-England Captain Ejected from Gatcombe"; "Horrible Hughes Insults Princess Anne – Career in Ruins".

I need not have worried. That's what being different class is all about. Her Royal Highness smiled at me, understood exactly what I was trying to say, and began talking about the humour in her life and in her sport.

"Eventing is so individual that there aren't the shared laughs that one probably experiences in other sports. Most of the things that have made me laugh are a result of some horrible mix-up or mistake – and actually some of those are decidedly unfunny. Once I was competing down in Devon and my horse noticed that there were deer in the surrounding park. He wouldn't do a thing. The dressage was so bad, with the horse trotting round as if he was on pogo sticks instead of legs, that eventually I had to laugh. That was similar to the time when I walked a course in two halves, doing half from the start and half from the finish. Unfortunately I missed the jump in the middle! So there I was, just about half way round and there's this gate in my way that I've never seen before. It's in those situations that you've got to laugh, if only to yourself.

"I suppose the funniest moments are fun for everyone else – but not for me. We won't mention the water jump." Take note, Emlyn.

"And what about your greatest moments Ma'am?"

"That's interesting. I know what I would like to say, namely completing the cross-country in the Olympics, but I can't say that because I can't remember it. I had a fall in the early part of the round and cannot, to this day, remember a thing about the rest of the cross-country. I suppose that my silver in the European Championships was my best performance, and the result which gives me most personal pride and satisfaction. Due to some late problems I was on a new horse, with virtually no time to get acquainted."

"How important is it, having a horse that you know and combine well with?"

"Eventing is about partnership. I've been very lucky with horses. Doublet was marvellous to ride; I think we all underestimated him a little. Goodwill was a very genuine horse. He was powerful too, and didn't need asking twice to do things. He would jump anything; I don't think there is a course in the world that he wouldn't take in his stride. But even the best horse can still act like a pig sometimes – it can be very difficult with a seriously uncooperative horse."

I recalled the size of the average eventing horse and wondered if this meant that, at times, men did have an unfair advantage over women. Results in the sport tend to suggest that it is one in which men and women compete on equal terms, but possibly that is not so.

"At times I have noticed that strength alone can control a horse. What happens though, is that women have to take a bit longer to get to know the horse. So women riders tend to have a better understanding in difficult situations whereas men will just rely upon their extra strength."

At this point the interview seemed to be back on the right path. But I still had one more chance to disgrace myself and my family. It started with a seemingly simple question: "Whom do you admire most today, or whom have you admired most in the past?"

"It's hard to say because who I think are good are not always those who have achieved most in terms of medals and championships. It's a matter of style as well as performance. Lucinda Green, of course, scores on both counts, and so does Virginia Leng. When it comes to the cross-country I am a particular admirer of Gillian Drawlson, a marvellous rider.

"As for the men? Well, there's Mark." I was anxious to show my knowledge of the modern eventing scene.

"Todd?" I mentioned the current favourite for the British Open.

"No," Her Royal Highness looked at me, smiling, "Mark, my husband." Emlyn, give up.

Of course, to take offence would be the very last thing The Princess Royal would do. Instead my mistake was passed off with a laugh and a smile, completely summing up the approach and style of this wonderful woman. I wished our interview could have gone on forever. Like me, The Princess Royal is happy to talk endlessly about sport. There is always so much to discuss, reminiscences to share, experiences to compare. Unfortunately, duty called and she had to go over to the main arena to present the awards at the end of the event for the Riding for the Disabled Association. Typically she was not going to be late for that.

The rest of the weekend, for both me and my family, was most enjoyable. Having spent the time recording what Her Royal Highness The Princess Royal had to say perhaps I ought to give the last word to her husband, Captain Mark Phillips. He came up to me at the evening party, took my arm and led me aside.

"Emlyn," he said in a serious tone. "I want you to promise never to invite me to appear on *A Question of Sport*!"

With such power, the boy from Barrow has come a long way.

Steve Davis

doing it by the book

Born in Romford, Essex, Steve Davis has won the World title on five occasions – 1981/'83/'84/'87/ '88. He has reached the final every year since 1983, losing on two occasions, in 1985 to Dennis Taylor and in 1986 to Joe Johnson. Since turning pro in 1978, he has won every ranking tournament and most of the unranked ones as well. He has won the UK Championship six times out of seven appearances since 1980. His annual income is £1 million, two-thirds of which is due to endorsements, advertising contracts and sponsorship. His hobbies include listening to rhythm and blues records in the Essex farmhouse which he shares with his parents.

The trappings of the modern world are supposed to make our lives easier. Car phones, jet aeroplanes, computers, FAX machines. . .the lot, have all held out the promise of increased leisure time and more efficiently organised working days. How come, then, I seem to spend most of my life either rushing from one place to another, or sitting in a traffic jam wishing I could rush from one place to anothë?

I think the answer is that we sometimes forget that men are not machines and we expect too much from ourselves and others. I'm always making the mistake of looking at two places on a motorway map, working out the miles in between and estimating how long it's going to take me. I still forget that motorways sometimes need to be repaired and that other people like to use the roads as well as me!

The reason for this little introduction is nothing to do with my campaign to do away with red cones, but to explain why my interview with the incomparable Steve Davis took place on the telephone. Steve is very like me in that he tries to pack a lot into his days. He is frequently to be seen working with one or two of his sponsors, he's very accommodating to the press and television stations for interviews and he's one of the most generous of stars when it comes to giving up time for charity functions and guest appearances. Oh yes, there's also a little matter of practising for hours every day and still finding the time to compete in tournaments and retain his position as the greatest snooker player in the world. With all this to contend with it's no wonder that some of the stars play their matches into the early hours!

I had met Steve on many occasions before mentioning the idea of the book to him. Of course, he's been a frequent visitor to my home town of Sheffield where the World Championships take place at the Crucible Theatre, and I'd also seen him on *A Question of Sport* and at a number of sporting events. I therefore assumed that a meeting would be no problem, but I was wrong. Comparing our diaries was like putting Liverpool up against Everton – they didn't match. It was either going to be a shouted interview across the central reservation of the M1 motorway, as he drove north and I went south (at least we'd both be in the outside lanes) or else it was going to be done on the 'phone. The 'phone idea won.

My friends at Radio Hallam fixed up the link, and got a tape running and I plunged into the interview:

"Hi, Steve." There was silence. I suddenly knew what is must be like to be reading the television news when a report you've just cued up doesn't materialise. "Helpless" is the word. Then, suddenly, there was a voice in the studio headphones.

"Hello Emlyn." I recognised the London accent immediately.

"Hi, Steve, how are you mate?"

"Hello Emlyn." He'd said that once.

"So, how's it going then?" I tried a different opening.

"Hello, Emlyn." Well I knew that Steve Davis wasn't thought to be the most exciting conversationalist in the world, but this was getting very dull indeed.

"Hello, Emlyn." He said it again. OK, so Steve wanted to say hello. Then I realised what I was holding in my hand. It was a note from the studio manager's assistant that read: "when you want to start, press the button marked 'Talk'". I pressed and was just in time to stop Steve saying "hello" to me again. He'd exhausted that line of conversation anyway.

"Hi, Steve." I found myself saying, getting into the swing of things straight from the start. "How are you keeping?" At this point I made a note to myself that being a radio interviewer wasn't as easy as it sounded.

Eventually, however, we worked out that we were both fine and that we were ready for the interview to commence. I knew a lot about Steve already but wanted to clear up one point first. When did it all start for him? I had heard or read some conflicting accounts of his early days with a cue.

"It was at Madison's Holiday Camp, St Mary's Bay, when I was fourteen that I first played on a full-size table and fell in love with the game. From that day on I only wanted to play snooker."

"And that was your first experience of the game?" I asked.

"No. I had been given a small table as a Christmas present when I was about eight." Perhaps this was the story I had heard before.

"And so you first started playing when you were eight, but progressed to the full-size table at fourteen?"

"Yes, but I've got a photograph of me holding a cue when I was three." Steve announced. Now I was getting confused again, and gave up trying to work out when that crucial first shot was made. But it must have been some time very early in Steve's life, somewhere on a small-sized table back in somebody's back parlour (do Cockneys have "back parlours"?). On that table, a very young boy took his first step towards a career that was going to make him not only the greatest player in the modern game but also a much-travelled millionaire. I wonder if he potted anything – he probably did.

And thinking about that first shot set me wondering when Steve first knew that he was going to reach the very top of his sport.

"Hard to say," replied Steve. "There's a difference between dreaming about cups and trophies and seriously thinking about winning them."

"Did you think, when you were fourteen and first played on the full sized table, that you were going to be as good as you later became?" I asked.

"You don't think in terms of ultimate success when you're that age. You can't know just how good you're going to be. I certainly had no concept of winning world championships or anything like that. I simply loved the game and wanted to play it as much as I could."

This comment also made me think. With the big money that is in snooker today, and in other sports like tennis and golf, do we still believe that the players love the game? Have we become so overwhelmed by the power of the pound sign that we believe all our sports stars are only in it for the money – for the "dosh" as Steve might say? There's no doubt that my "Great Britons" all loved their respective sports. They were there because they enjoyed it – take the money away and Steve Davis would still be the world's number one. The fact that Steve started playing in an age where there was almost no money at all is proof enough – if proof was needed – of what I'm saying.

And in that age, the early days of the television show *Pot Black*, but before the era of the blanket coverage of the World Championships and other major tournaments, who was Steve's hero? My assumption, knowing one or two other players, was that Steve fell under the spell of John Spencer.

"Ray Reardon" came the answer. "The reason I liked him at the time," Steve continued, "was because he was a winner; in fact he was *the* winner in those days. I first saw him at an annual tournament at a Pontin's Holiday Camp. That was one of the biggest events around at the time and I remember sitting at the back being overawed by the man."

Snooker has come a long way in a few short years. No disrespect to Pontin's Holiday Camps, but can you imagine them now hosting one of the major tournaments?

"And was Ray the major influence on your early career?" I continued my questioning, imagining that British Telecom might pull the plug on us at any minute.

"In one respect, yes, but I also owe a lot to the great Joe Davis."

"Did you watch him too?"

"No, I never saw him in his prime. I'm a bit too young for that, you know. He was important to me because I learned to play the game using his book!"

Steve had to be kidding. Sitting in a radio studio in Sheffield was not the best way to conduct an interview because I couldn't see if Steve was taking the mick or not. But surely he had to have his fingers crossed when he said that – the greatest snooker player in the world learned how to play from a book. It's the same as suggesting that Margaret Thatcher got her job after watching *Yes Prime Minister*. (I won't say any more than that in case I offend one of my heroes, but you know what I mean.)

I think Steve sensed my incredulity, even over the 'phone link. "It's perfectly true" he continued. "My Dad and I had this book and we would follow it page by page. We'd check on the theory of a particular aspect of the game, read it up, talk about it, and then I would go and practise. We did this for my entire basic game. I'm not saying that we took every word as law, but we certainly used the book for ground work. We used to say that I was like putty and my Dad, with Joe's help, was there to mould me into a player.

"I'm not ashamed to say that I had no instinctive flair as a young player. But I think this helped, because there was nothing getting in the way of me learning a very solid basic game. With this under my belt, I could then proceed to learn the tricks of the trade, gain the experience I needed and, also, allow my own skills to come out a little more."

"And you used a book?"

"Yes."

I knew Steve was telling the truth because he never told me the title of the volume. He's too intent on staying at the top to give any secrets away. For me, book learning would never have done, but I suppose that snooker, much like other intensely personal games such as golf, can be helped by working closely on the fundamentals. In football, no amount of reading up could help you when your team mates mucked it up, or your opponents played out of their skins. But with the solo sports, where a brilliant pot from behind the black or a thirty foot putt from the edge of the green can turn a match, matters are very different. Of course, no amount of book learning can prepare you for the pressures of the major competitions, and so how did Steve make the transition from local tables, with his book tucked in his pocket, to the big time and his first professional tournaments? Did he, for example, know then that he was going to be the best?

"No. And I'm very sure about that. I remember my sentiments when I first turned pro and started getting into the big tournaments and exhibitions. I thought it would be a great opportunity for me to play against the top players and, as a result, my game would improve. I'm not trying to sound unduly modest, but, at first, I didn't see myself reaching anywhere near the top. I just wanted to improve.

"This actually worked against me in many of my early matches. I thought, because I had become a professional, that I would suddenly have to turn it on. I looked for every possible means of improving my game, forgetting the very skills that had brought me to this position in the first place. It wasn't until I began to relax in the company of other players that I started to put a few results together."

"Did you take any real pastings in those early days?" You can ask questions like that if you're sitting two hundred miles away from the man you're interviewing.

"Not really, I'm happy to say, but Ray did turn me over once and I've never forgotten it. It was only the second or third time I'd played him and it was still such an unbelievable thrill for me to be at the same table as my childhood hero. But I was determined not to be overawed and had the right attitude. It was a round robin competition with two groups of four players, the winner from each going to play in the final. In my group I had won and drawn my best-of-four-frames matches and knew that I needed to get one frame from the four against Ray to qualify for the final. I knew I could do it. . .and lost four–nil! It was the first time I'd been in front and had the feeling of looking over my shoulder at the rest of the pack. I enjoyed that sensation and it didn't hold any fears for me only, on that occasion, it didn't last for long. Ray simply pulled out all the tricks to beat me. Of course he played very well, but he also unsettled me by chatting to me when I was trying to concentrate, by frequently asking for chalk to be wiped off the cue ball, for colours to be re-spotted and so on. Nothing in particular, but everything together, led to me losing my bottle I suppose."

"But did it help you in the long term?" I asked this with my own experiences very much in mind. If somebody made me look a fool on the pitch, or if a team put one over on Liverpool, which I'm happy to say wasn't that often, I'd first feel sick about it – and then want to profit by the experience. Sometimes later that day, if I could bear it, or more likely with the lads on the following day, I'd chew over what went wrong and prepare, both mentally and physically, for the same eventuality. Also, and this is very important, defeat always made me feel so bad that each time it happened I vowed would be the last. It didn't quite work out that way but I do believe that all great sports stars have got to hate losing; without that they're never going to reach the top. But back to my question Steve – did it help?

"Yes. It made me stronger. I like to recall an incident that occurred shortly after my defeat by Ray. I was playing in a match with the very experienced referee John Williams in control. I had just potted the pink, following a red, and John had to take the pink out of the pocket to re-spot it. It's something that must come automatically to him, having done the same action countless times before. But this was the one that got away. To my surprise he coolly walked over to the cue ball and picked it up, moving towards the pink spot with it in his hand. My opponent quickly saw what was going on, and claimed four points to himself. For some reason he reckoned I had played a foul shot.

"My first response was to argue my case and point out exactly what had happened. But I saw that the conflict was going to be between my opponent and John. Rather than get involved I excused myself and went to the toilet. When I came back the incident had been resolved, the discussions had died down, and most importantly, my concentration was intact. It's small moments like that that keep the experienced pros on top when their less illustrious opponents might be playing a blinder."

In telling this story I noticed that Steve didn't mention the other player's name. Of course he knew it, but I knew Steve well enough to know that he wouldn't want to say anything that was critical of another player. However, I thought I'd give him the chance to break his gentlemanly code and asked him whom he least liked playing – and why.

"There's nobody really, but some people do take a lot of getting used to." Steve was not to be drawn, and good for him.

"What about Alex Higgins? Does he pose any special problems because, like it or not, he's a special sort of player?"

"He hasn't bothered me because, in a strange way, I've been concerned about myself and my own ability. Before a major match I'm always worrying about how well I'll perform; this tends to stop me thinking too much about my opponents. There was a stage in my career when I used to get very keyed up over playing Tony Meo. He was the big cheese on the London circuit, where I didn't play much, and everywhere I went I'd hear how well he was doing. I think I've conquered that now." I could almost see Steve's smile as he said this.

I didn't want to draw Steve on his opinions of others, that would really be unfair – and anyway Steve would be unlikely to spill the beans – but there was one topic I wanted to raise with him about the Hurricane, Alex Higgins. I wondered if it ever bothered Steve that Alex was hailed as "the people's champion" and yet it was Steve who won everything.

"No, I can't say it matters to me although I know it upset some of those around me. Saying he's the people's champion suggests not only that he's the champion, something that can be readily disproved, but that he's the one the fans really like. Maybe he is, but I don't like the implication that he's in touch with "the people" and players like me are stand-offish or aloof. I don't think that's true. Without wanting to appear too cocky I think I suffer from the same problem as somebody like Ivan Lendl. He's got to the top of his profession by playing very well and winning more tournaments than anybody else. But because he doesn't chuck his racket around, doesn't wait until the last minute to pull off a sensational win and doesn't clown around when he's in a match. . .he's not popular with the press or public. I've got some wonderful fans, but I know that I'm not as highly thought of as some other players who haven't got half of my record."

89

It was sad to hear Steve say this, although I don't suppose he loses any sleep over it. I suppose it's a peculiarly British trait. We long for sporting success and exhort our youngsters to do well and take on the world. Then, when they've reached the top and are the envy of the world, we turn off them a bit. Thinking about tennis again, I wonder if we Brits would have taken to Martina Navratilova (had she been a British champion) as much as Virginia Wade. I somehow doubt it.

Perhaps Steve has become just too good. I don't expect any American readers to understand that, but that's the problem you face if you're British. If you've reached the top, you've just got to be knocked down.

Time was running out, and the 'phone bill was running up. I asked Steve about the game of snooker, and about its future. Could it get any bigger?

"Not in the UK. But the growth has got to come worldwide. The Far East has become a big area but the main goal is, of course, America. The potential audience is so great, but I'm sceptical about the prospects. Just because some other sports have taken off there it doesn't necessarily follow that snooker will do so too."

"And Steve, I have to ask this," this introduction was by way of preparation for a Hughes silly question. "Do you have any ambitions?" Considering he's won everything, at least twice over, what could he say?

"In terms of tournament victories I just want to go on winning. It's the old cliché but I'll take each as it comes, and give each my best shot. But more generally I want to become the Jack Nicklaus of snooker. Not just to be the best for a short period, but to win and win again. And then come back and win some more."

I thought of Steve now, as a young man, and tried to picture him as the grand old man of the sport. Perhaps in twenty years' time, with a dozen World Championships to his name. Who knows? I certainly think he's got the temperament for it. Did he think he had what it takes?

"Yes. My temperament is sound. Of course, under the calm exterior I'm sometimes very churned up. But I can control it, most of the time."

These last few words put me in mind of his defeat by Joe Johnston in the World Championship final; he didn't seem to be very calm that night. In fact it was the only time I can recall ever seeing Steve appear to be in a panic. I mentioned this, again feeling bold because of the 'phone line separating us.

"Emlyn, could Liverpool lose to Wimbledon?" Thanks for reminding me; I'd only just got over that. The worst part was my unpremeditated attack on our milkman for whistling the Wombles song. "Of course not," Steve continued, "but they did.

"And the reason was that they were so shocked by the goal, and the

90

thought of defeat, that they couldn't recover their composure. It was the same for me. I was so shocked by the thought of defeat that I became almost frozen. I'd lost to Dennis Taylor before in the final, on the last black, but that was not the same. Defeat could have been anticipated and I coped with it. Against Joe, it was awful and I did lose my control.

"I have to tell you also about a match you probably didn't see. Against Tony Knowles, I lost 10–1. I was so bad. You'd have laughed at me that day Em. In fact I had to laugh in the end, it was just terrible. But happily I've avoided too many shocks like that. Once a decade will be enough for me."

"Final question then Steve," I was getting the wind-up sign from the other studio. "Tell me about your manager, Barry Hearn."

"He's become a great friend, and that's the best compliment I can pay him. On top of that, of course, he's created my career for me and is my number one fan."

That fact was self-evident from a recent quote from Barry following Steve's receipt of an MBE. When asked how he felt about it, Barry replied, honestly and simply, "It's about time too." Hear, hear.

But for this interview I'll leave the last words not to Steve's manager but to the man himself. I put this in in case there's anybody reading this who still believes that Steve is a little reserved or lacking in a sense of humour. I thanked Steve for his time and told him about the plans for the book.

"I've got a book coming out at Christmas too, you know. It's called *The Steve Davis Book of How to be Really Interesting.*"

"Don't tell me Steve, it's only got two pages."

"No, Em, this is *really* interesting. It's got three."

John Francome

the professional amateur

Champion jockey seven times, West Country-born John Francome is recognised as one of the greatest ever National Hunt riders. His record 1036 winners, many for the famous Fred Winter yard he joined in 1969, stands as a testament to his ability and courage. Although he never won the Grand National as a jockey, the racing world now awaits his appearance at Aintree as the winning trainer – a new career he has taken to as naturally as he took to riding.

John Francome, champion National Hunt jockey seven times, winner of more races than anyone else in the history of his sport; a popular and affable man, famous for his good looks and raffish manner; now retired from riding, and a successful trainer (and author!). . .and I've got to confess he used to annoy me.

Why was this? Well, before I confronted him with my complaint, I wanted to find out a little more about one of the most popular jockeys of modern racing. For instance, where did it all start?

"On the beach, on the back of a donkey." John's West Country burr is at once captivating and friendly. "My granny would take me down to Barry Island in South Wales during the holidays. It had to be the donkeys for me. And they gave me the taste for riding that led to my interest in show jumping."

John actually competed with the Great Britain show jumping team and won a gold medal in the European Championships. And from a natural ability in the saddle, perhaps it's not surprising that he moved on to racing over the sticks. His first contact with the sport was as a part of Fred Winter's Uplands stable. Was it a deliberate move to try to get in with one of the most successful trainers around?

"To tell the truth," which is something John does most of the time – and which sometimes gets him into trouble, "I'd never even heard of him!

"I just said to my parents that I wanted to have a go at racing and they suggested writing to the great man. To give him his credit, there were, or are today, very few trainers who would take on somebody like I was then. No experience in racing and no real knowledge of the sport; all I had was a love of horses and the need to train for something at which I might be able to make a living.

"I fired off this ridiculously immodest letter and was rewarded with an interview and a two-month trial."

"And so was it all plain sailing from there?" I asked John.

"No. In fact my career was nearly over before it had begun. I had decided to hand my notice in and went to see Fred Winter, the 'Governor', complete with letter of resignation. I had even 'phoned my parents to tell them to expect me home at the weekend. When I turned up at the office it was only to discover that he was away for the day, out playing golf. So I pocketed my letter, thinking that it could wait for tomorrow. In the meantime, however, I was told to take a horse called Osbaldeston out schooling because I would be riding him in a race for conditional jockeys the following week."

John held on to his letter – and held on to Osbaldeston as the partnership went on to win several races. A brilliant career had been launched and perhaps a clue given as to why John called his own autobiography *Born Lucky*.

Thinking about John and his career-long relationship with Fred Winter put me in mind of the relationship I had enjoyed with Bill Shankly while I was playing at Liverpool. Was it the same for John as it had been for me, working under the guidance of one of the acknowledged "greats" in the game? This was something that intrigued me as I had received so many differing answers about the way in which the teacher–pupil situation works in sport at the highest level. Was George Best better for the influence of Matt Busby? Would the world ever have heard of Steve Davis without the work of Barry Hearn? Did John Francome become champion jockey because of Fred Winter?

"Fred and I got on well, by keeping our distance. The only real advice he gave me was on how to hold and use the stick in racing. He also put me right when I made a mistake, and I took it upon myself never to make the same mistake again.

"I think his greatest asset was in knowing what it was like to be a jockey. He knew that things couldn't go right all the time and so was always ready to commiserate with you if you had a touch of bad luck. Also he understood when to leave you alone. Jockeys don't want trainers on their backs. I used to ride out with him and we hardly said a thing to each other. I can remember car trips to meetings when we wouldn't exchange more than twenty words the whole time. But one was always aware of his interest and commitment – and he always gave you confidence. There's nothing worse than a jockey with no self-assurance. Lack of confidence is bad for the jockey, the horse, and even other mounts in a race. The Governor never left you short on confidence. Basically, though, I never told him how to train and he never told me how to ride."

In football, of course, it's possible to learn a lot on one's own, playing in unsupervised matches and simply kicking a ball about. Racing, though, has to be different. The jockey needs proper races before he can begin to acquire the necessary skill and experience. How did John manage to learn his trade if Fred Winter wasn't the teacher?

"I was largely self-taught, and I learned by watching. When I was show jumping it was Harvey Smith and David Broome. Later, once into racing, I used to watch such experts as David Mould and Jeff King. I learned a lot from them, unfortunately not nearly enough to allow me to beat them on more than the odd occasion."

By this point in our chat I had really warmed to John Francome. Somehow he infuses everybody with enthusiasm and he seems to bring a sense of fun to every topic. But I hadn't forgotten the bone I wished to pick with him – only I decided to wait a little longer before challenging him.

Like some of the other top sports stars I've met in the course of writing this book, I can see similarities between him and me, and I can also see great differences. His attitude is one of dedication, ambition and single-mindedness, and yet, somehow, he doesn't seem to be too affected by disappointment. If you asked me what was the worst thing in football then I'd have to say "losing". Ask John and the answer is likely to be "the loos at Fontwell". But is it all a façade, is he really that laid back about the whole thing? My feeling is that John is what I would call a professional amateur. His professionalism comes out in his hard work, his dedicated approach and his ability to be consistent in the saddle, year after year. The amateur in him tells him that defeat doesn't really matter, that tomorrow is another day and that he can always go and do something else because, after all, it's only a sport anyway. But why try to analyse the man when he was sitting there in front of me and more than capable of speaking his own mind?

"Of course, winning is what you're there for," John began when I put my next question to him, "but there are plenty of times when you know that your mount isn't really in with a chance. You do your best and hope for the best, but it's no good getting bothered about losing."

"But to win the Jockeys' Championship seven times suggests that you really wanted it."

"The truth is that after the first one, which I really did want to win, it was a case of not wanting to lose it. That might sound funny but that's exactly how I felt. I didn't wake up worrying about how John Francome was going to win the Championship, but I did have nightmares about somebody else winning it instead of me! I think there's a difference."

"But did you find that the winning got easier?" I asked John this because, at Liverpool, we always found that it was easier to win something for a second or third time; the first time was always the hardest. I don't quite know why this was but I think it's got a lot to do with confidence – and the fact that other teams get a bit more resigned to losing to you. If you're going to lose to Hartlepool United then that's the worst thing that can possibly happen; you'd fight like mad to prevent that happening. But if you lose to Liverpool, well, so have plenty of other teams so is it such a big problem?

"It actually got harder after my first Championship." John's answer surprised me. "The main reason was that I couldn't get the rides I needed. You don't win the National Hunt Championship by picking and choosing a few choice mounts. You have to race, day in day out, all over the country and in all kinds of races. Of course I got a lot of rides from Fred Winter's yard but I needed a whole lot more to fill my schedule. Trainers tended not to call me because they thought that either I wouldn't want to ride their mounts or else that I would be too expensive. Before the Championship I used to spend hours 'phoning round getting rides; after the Championship I was still spending the same amount of time.

"I would read the racing press with the four-day declarations, look around at what was up and coming and start the business of contacting trainers. I have to put in a small advertisement here for car 'phones. A jockey's life can be a whole lot easier with one of those magic machines. In fact, right up until my last day in the saddle I was still ringing round for rides on a daily basis."

Listening to John mention his "last day in the saddle" inevitably set me thinking about his dramatic decision to quit on what could, I suppose, be described as his "last day *out* of the saddle". It was at Chepstow, in the middle of a meeting and the middle of a race, when the aptly named The Reject decided that he would both throw John off and proceed to walk all over him. John saw the writing on the wall, walked back into the weighing room, found someone to take his remaining mounts for the afternoon – and quit. Why so sudden?

"I told Fred at the beginning of the 1984–85 season that it was going to be my last, but at the time I thought I would ride through to the end. On that April day, after the fall, I just thought that I had had enough; even one more ride would be tempting fate. I had been very lucky the month before at Cheltenham when I seriously thought I could have died. I came off over a jump and got tangled up in the irons. It was the fact that I managed to hold on to the reins, and that the leather held, that prevented me from being dragged all round the damned course. I don't even like to imagine how it could have ended up." I didn't, either.

Dramatic though the mercurial Francome's decision to quit was, the legend of Francome was really crowned by the events surrounding the Jockeys' Championship of 1982–83. Towards the end of the campaign Peter Scudamore was about twenty winners ahead of Francome. It was then that the Championship race leader broke his arm. It was a bad break that necessitated a plate being inserted to help the healing process. The history books tell us that Francome drew level at the top of the table with just a couple of days of the season left. . .and then decided to shut up shop for the year, thus sharing the Championship and honourably declining to profit by his rival's unfortunate accident. The Championship was shared and the British sporting public acclaimed a gentleman and a champion.

Nobody would have begrudged John an outright win in the Championship. Sport is all about lucky and unlucky breaks (excuse the unintentional pun) and for Peter Scudamore it would have been "just one of those things". So what was it that encouraged John to be so magnanimous?

97

"Partly it was the thought of Peter sitting there in hospital watching "his" Championship evaporating. It seemed very hard on him, especially since I had already won it a couple of times and Peter never had. But there was also the competitive element. I was sitting in the weighing room when the news broke about Peter. I immediately said to those around me that I would now have a chance to catch him. The other jockeys, whom we'll not name except to say that one of them was called Steve Smith Eccles, said I'd be lucky to get twenty more rides that season, let alone twenty more winners. That was all the encouragement I needed to go out there and prove them wrong.

"Really, though, I was very happy to share the Championship with Scud, but I'd like to record that he still owes me £400 for my share of the prize!"

Listening to John, and noticing the glances he kept getting from other people in the restaurant, it was not hard to see why the British have taken him to their hearts. But being a handsome hero is not always enough; there needs to be that something extra. Whatever it is, John has it in abundance. For example, he's popular with the public because he's often unpopular with those in authority, and there's nothing we like more than the man who stands up to officialdom. I wondered, though, if his brushes with stewards and other officials were a part of the real story or just the invention of the media.

"Let me give you an example," John began. "In my last year I was fined £2500 for not riding out a horse, Easter Lee, into second place at Newbury. I had knocked spots off him and he was knackered. Twenty yards from the post I dropped my hands and another horse came and did me right on the line. I was dead unlucky.

"I know rules are rules but they have no idea just what £2500 means. It's the equivalent of riding in forty novice chases on a Monday at Leicester, and I can tell you there's only one word to describe a twenty-six horse novice chase at Leicester – terrifying.

"Of course, stewards are amateurs and maybe only get to officiate at a few days racing every year. Perhaps it's not surprising that they sometimes make mistakes. But it seems that sometimes they haven't even been watching the race.

"I remember once at Plumpton, on the favourite, I had a really bad fall. It turned me upside down and I finished covered in mud from head to toe. A steward came up to me and, as is traditional, addressed me by my surname: 'Francome, we want to see you.' When I asked him why he said: 'We want to see why you pulled that horse up.' I just looked at him, flabbergasted, as if to say: 'What do you think this lot is, designer mud?' They hadn't even noticed what had happened. Such matters may be isolated but they still occur."

You get the feeling that John would have been happier riding in unsupervised races, perhaps in an age before the present when video cameras weren't scanning a field of runners and where it was a case of every man for himself. Certainly some of the stories he tells tend to glorify the rather wilder days of steeplechasing.

One story in particular concerned former jockey Pat Buckley who had been edged through the wing of a fence and out of the race. Buckley had parted company and was generally none too happy. A couple of weeks later Buckley and the other rider involved in the incident came up against each other again. As the pack of horses was rounding a bend Buckley found himself alongside his old adversary. Deftly, he reached across and snatched the horse's bridle shouting, as he did so: "Let's see you ride that bugger out!".

Although John did admit that he really was pleased that riding had become a lot safer in recent years, he still delighted in telling this story:

"There was a real old character of the courses called Frenchie Nicholson. One day he was lying second last in a nothing sort of race. As he was nearing the finish he cut across the horse that was in last place, sending the nag into the rails and the jock over them. It caused a few bumps and bruises to the rider but no lasting damage. Back in the weighing room the rider asked Frenchie why he had done such a thing. Frenchie thought for a moment and then delivered the one-word reply: 'Practice'."

Francome, as a bold, fearless and sometimes impudent rider, clearly likes such tales. I wondered if he missed all the banter of the weighing room, a haven for jockeys and their valets where owners and trainers are not allowed. He is now a trainer and obviously looks at the racing game from a slightly different perspective. I also wondered if he was in the right frame of mind for the question I had been saving up. I decided to start with the questions about training first.

"What do you miss about riding?" I asked.

"Nothing really, because training keeps me busy. I thought I might at first, because riders, particularly over the sticks, are a friendly and fairly close-knit bunch. I mean, there's absolutely no good getting cocky about your achievements in front of the other guys because you've just as much chance of landing on your backside as they have in the next race. And there's always going to be the moment when you rely on another jockey to take his mount round you rather than through you after a fall.

"But as it has turned out, I've come across an equally pleasant crowd in the owners and others who are associated with my stables."

"And how do you compare the two jobs?"

"I worry a lot more about the training than I did about the riding. But

I've found that the basic rules still operate. Do your best and be honest; and it pays in the long run. For example, although it's easier to tell an owner that you think his horse has got great potential and that it's sure to achieve success, it's better to be honest and tell him that he's unlikely ever to win much or repay his fees. In the long term this can only help your relationships with people.

"Also I've found that I have to be honest about working with people. I've turned down a couple of offers to train because I knew I couldn't get on with the guy. Within weeks or months we would be at each other, needling and nagging. I can do without that.

"What else? I've found out that one thing remains the same, no matter what branch of racing you're in. When you think things can't get worse – they do. I ran a horse called Crimson Knight at Worcester and fully expected him to be my first winner. He was twenty lengths clear coming to the second last when he fell. That's the game and you accept it, but it was a bitter blow. I 'phoned the owner and set off home. The first thing to greet me on my return was a call from the lad saying that Crimson Knight, although he had appeared OK when I saw him, had, in fact, punctured a lung and had been destroyed. I was so shocked and the owner was devastated. It was around the time of my first book and I was tempted to rename it: *Born Unlucky*."

As we approached the end of our discussion, bringing the John Francome story up to date, I realised I'd got to challenge John with my problem. Since we'd already paid the bill for the meal, I'd nothing to lose.

"John," I began nervously. "I must admit that you really annoyed me at times during your career." There's nothing like coming straight to the point I decided. "More than once I've had money riding on you and you've been interviewed about the prospects for the forthcoming race. I've watched the television, needing my confidence boosting because I don't like throwing fifty pence away willy nilly, and you've come out and said that you thought the horse had some chance, but then again it might not stay and could fall. All I needed was you to say that it was a cert and nothing was going to beat it, and you come out with this stuff about 'maybe it could' and 'if all goes well'. Explain yourself."

"Honesty, Emlyn," was John's predictable answer, "and a sense of proportion. It's no good promising the world if you know you can't deliver."

"Yes, I see that, but I've never known a top sports star yet who wasn't brim full of confidence. I know footballers who could be lining up with ten blind guys against Barcelona and they reckon they've got an even chance."

"It's not lack of confidence, Emlyn, just a realistic view of the situation.

It's a race we're talking about, and a lot can happen between the off and the post. And, I'm sorry if you're fifty pence out of pocket because of me!"

I suppose it was the professional amateur in John that was showing through again. That he has fierce ambition and an iron determination is undeniable, but ultimately he's not going to lose sight of what life is all about – and racing can only be one (very large) part of that life.

John is a keen tennis player, a dabbler in various businesses, he lives in a house he built himself and, most recently, he's become a successful novelist. He's also great company. And, if ever he says that one of his horses has even an outside chance you know you're talking racing certainties – I'd even stretch to a pound for one of them.

Mike Gatting

the hardest job in sport

Mike Gatting, "Gatts", has played cricket for Middlesex since 1975. He made his Test debut in 1977 at the age of twenty, taking over from David Gower as England captain in 1986. He started successfully – retaining the Ashes and leading England to victory in the World Series and the Perth Challenge. In the 1987 World Cup in India, he led England to the final where they lost to Australia. He is one of the top batsmen in the country, having made almost 20,000 runs in his career. In recognition of his dedication to his sport, he was awarded the OBE in 1987.

*S*ubdued. That's the only word I can think of to describe Mike Gatting when I met him. For all I know he may have been suffering from a heavy night out. I suspect, however, that the problems that go along with being captain of England were preying rather heavily on his mind. As David Coleman said when I talked to him, if you're writing something today for publishing in a few months' time, don't mention the current England cricket captain – because it will probably be out-of-date information.

I'm not going to get involved with the politics of cricket, as I make a point of not discussing politics of any kind. (The only time I let my guard slip was when I once gave Robert Maxwell a hard time on a television chat show; I suppose he must have forgiven me for I still write for the *Daily Mirror*.) All I want to say, by way of introduction to this piece on Mike, is that being captain of your country is the greatest honour you can have.

The biggest thrill for me was pulling on an England shirt for the first time. But being made captain of the team, a job I held through four managers, was my greatest honour. You can't get any higher. You start off playing in junior level, get your first break in a League team, join a top club, win major honours and get picked for your country. But there's one job that tops the lot – captain. And they can never take it away from you. When I speak at dinners I'm often flatteringly introduced as "star of *A Question of Sport*", "winner of countless medals", "captain of Liverpool", etc. The title that really pleases me, though, is "captain of England".

I hope Mike never forgets this. When people start to question his decisions or write the occasional silly piece in the papers, he should remember that *he* was picked to be captain of England. The people holding the daggers weren't.

Enough of this. I'm beginning to talk in terms of disappointment and criticism. We can never forget that Mike Gatting led the most successful sortie Down Under of any England captain. For all true Brits, 1986/7 was a most satisfying winter. The Test series wrapped up when we weren't given much of a chance, and the clean sweep of the one-day international tournaments made for marvellous late-night television. The voices of choked Australian commentators and the sight of losing West Indian teams will live in the memory for a long time. That was followed up by the fantastic campaign for the World Cup, held in India and Pakistan in 1987. That was a classic case of so near yet so far. To beat the Indians in the semi-final was one of our greatest one-day triumphs. And having gloated about Australian defeats a few moments ago, I'm happy to congratulate them on their victory in the final. It was an incredible achievement, made possible by good team work, plenty of effort and a captain who instilled pride and belief in his players. In my book there's a lot of similarity between Allan Border, the Australian skipper, and Mike Gatting.

Perhaps the most striking comparison is that neither Gatts nor Border comes from the old-school-tie mould. Remembering, again, David Coleman's assessment, Gatting is a sergeant-major not a commissioned officer. My first question was intended to uncover the background that led to Mike's current position in the game.

"For a lad keen on sports, I had the perfect upbringing. My parents were stewards of a sports ground in Hendon. There were all the facilities you could wish for. Steve, my younger brother by two years, and I would play for hours, mostly football, before diving in the big plunge bath in the pavilion. It was football at first because that was the easiest thing for two youngsters to play amongst themselves. In the summer, though, we'd watch the cricketers and bowl at the batsmen before their innings or borrow their bats to knock up in the nets.

"Like so many other kids our age we'd play as often as possible. We were quite useful and so got picked for various representative sides. One thing led to another. In cricket terms it was a steady progression from county schoolboy trials to the Middlesex schoolboys' team. I also represented England at under-fifteen and under-seventeen level. All along, however, I think my heart was in football."

"Where did the parting of the ways come? What made you decide to play cricket?" I asked.

"It wasn't a difficult decision in the end. Steve was having trials with Arsenal and was eventually asked to sign on. I was on Watford's books; they were then in the Third Division. The choice for me was between the reserve or junior side of a Third Division soccer team or playing cricket for one of the top county sides, Middlesex. I felt I had a good chance of making the grade at Middlesex as I had already played for their Colts and Young Cricketer sides and I also thought I would enjoy it more. Had I been the one to have been offered terms with Arsenal my decision may have been different."

So many top sports stars seem to be able to play well at more than one sport. Alan Hansen who followed me at Liverpool is one I remember well; he was a top squash player in Scotland. J.P.R. Williams from Welsh rugby's hall of fame represented his country at tennis. And Mike Gatting? Could he have made the grade at soccer? His positive attitude is certainly right for the game.

I suspected, however, that it was more than just a simple decision of football or cricket. I wondered if there were other influences at work.

"I had good coaches, especially in Ted Jackson and Peter Ferrara, and I also went away for a course at Lilleshall. That really set me thinking about the game; it was also good fun, being away from home for the first time."

"And who were your early heroes?"

"Basil D'Oliveira I especially remember. You could always rely upon him to come up with a couple of vital wickets or a lower-order stand. I admired that kind of determination and concentration. Of course, the problem of playing a lot of cricket is that you don't get to watch much. My friends were always talking about the top players of Middlesex and England and I had hardly ever seen them play. I had to make a special point of going along to watch some matches at Lord's. This was a crucial part of the learning process.

"I remember seeing Fred Titmus in action one evening, bowling against Gordon Greenidge. Greenidge had already made a few runs and there were about twenty minutes of the day's play left. Most bowlers would have been content to wind down the day with a couple of tight maiden overs. Most batsmen would have been thankful for the opportunity to play them out. But Fred couldn't play like that and he had to tease and tempt Greenidge. He was out, stumped, at twenty-five minutes past six!"

Mike's voice gave away his enthusiasm for the game and the obvious thrill that he experienced being a youngster on Middlesex's books. The subdued Mike I had greeted some time before was gone. Gatts was now exhibiting his normal forthright and ebullient character.

I remember the way I had felt as a youngster with Blackpool. I recall those days with pride, but with some embarrassment too. My enthusiasm for the game used to spill over into other aspects of life as a professional footballer. On one occasion, after I'd been at Blackpool for all of two weeks, we were taken out for a day's golf. I had never been on a golf course before so had no idea how to behave or what to do.

I was on the tee, about to drive, when Jimmy Armfield, then captain of Blackpool and England, walked across the fairway. He was with a couple of players and, as captain, a couple of club officials. I was so excited by the whole thing that I shouted out: "Hey, isn't this great!" I felt such a fool, but I couldn't be any other way. It was unnatural for me to keep my excitement to myself. Had Mike experienced anything similar? I asked him this because I suspected we were two of a kind in our enthusiasm for sport and our unintentional disregard for convention.

"When I hear the name 'Tadge' Webster," explained Mike, "I still feel a shiver of embarrassment.

"He was very well known in Middlesex and held important committee positions. Everybody knew him as 'Tadge'. I first met him at some function and he kindly came over to me and welcomed me to the county. 'Thank you Tadge,' was my response. As I said it I could almost hear the intake of breath around the room. Total horror at the young upstart.

"I forget who it was who put me right on that occasion but it was probably Ian Gould. Ian took me under his wing from an early date and showed me the ropes, told me what and whom to look out for and generally how to behave in the new company I was keeping. I'm told I was a little raw as a youngster although I only saw it as natural enthusiasm. Gouldie also had footballing aspirations so we shared a common language."

I had trouble imagining the life of the young cricketer on the first rungs of the professional ladder. Could it be the same as for an apprentice in football? The life of an apprentice is certainly unlike any other I know, although things may be changing a bit now, but when I was at Blackpool we did all the "housework" of the club. This meant cleaning the boots, helping with the pitch from time to time, sweeping out the changing rooms and painting anything that stood still long enough – except our left back. None of those jobs mattered to us, providing we got our training and matches in. After all, we were professional footballers. I would have cut the pitch with nail clippers if they'd asked me. I explained this to Mike.

"The cricket system is a bit different. The only place we were treated differently was in the nets. We'd normally get in last, and occasionally have to stay on later to do a bit of extra bowling to first-team members."

"During this time did you ever have any doubts about whether you would make it or not? When did you first know that you had what it took?" I asked Mike this because I've sometimes noticed that a little stroke of luck, a little piece of good advice can make all the difference.

"Nothing happened in particular. It was a step-by-step progression. In 1975 I was seventeen and played my first match for Middlesex. By 1976 I was a fairly regular member of the side, played for my bowling and my batting, and in 1977 I went on a Young England trip to the West Indies. This seemed to me to be ideal progress."

"And was it plain sailing from then on?"

"No. In fact things went badly for a while. I became better known for my batting and was recognised as an opener. I thought I had settled into a regular spot but then my form went completely. Mike Smith and Roland Butcher were doing well and I found myself back in the second eleven. From being a regular in the county side, and after touring with the Young England team, I found this hard to cope with. I didn't know how to react because cricket was my life and I had been making such good progress. Suddenly to be out of it left me rather bewildered.

"In those situations, though, you can only grit your teeth and try to play yourself out of it. Don Bennett was the coach who looked after the second eleven at the time. He made me captain for a representative match against a Young South Africa side. Steve, my brother, was playing in the game and he and I went in together at, I think, numbers three and four. I was so determined that I hardly spoke for my first half-hour at the crease. Then I got a few runs under my belt and wanted to show people that I was ideal captain material. I kept giving advice to the batsman at the other end. Unfortunately it was my own brother who wasn't having any of it. At lunch he spoke to Don and said he'd refuse to go out again unless the captain was told to shut up and allow other players to get on with their own game.

"Because I knew so much depended on that game I was probably more nervous than ever before. The second eleven, around that time, had so many good players in it that the standard of cricket was high. I played a lot of my early cricket with John Emburey in the second eleven. Larry Gomes too was making the grade around then."

Mike mentioned two players who had made it into the first-class game from their origins in the second eleven. But for almost every player who does come through the ranks, another two or three fall by the wayside. As I mentioned earlier, this is often because of some bad luck, poor advice or just not being in the right place at the right time. Who knows what talent has been lost to the sporting world for these reasons. I can remember seeing young lads on the books at both Blackpool and Liverpool who I thought were certain to be future stars. I can't even recall their names now. Had they just made the right move when the talent scout was watching, or if the player they were understudying had been injured at a crucial period, maybe they would be writing this book today.

I put this point to Mike. Was there a moment, around the time of his relegation to the second eleven, when the name of Gatting could have been lost to the cricket world?

"I don't think so, because I was very determined to get back straight away. But I do understand what you mean. It worked out for me. I got a few runs in the match I've just mentioned and found myself back in the first team pretty quickly. If I needed any further encouragement it was in one of my first games back, against Essex. Smithy and Butch were still opening and I was batting at number eight. The Essex lads, who always enjoy their cricket, gave me such stick. As I took guard they were saying things like: 'Here comes the tail' and 'Gatts must have become an all-rounder then.' That stung me into action.

"On the business of failing to make the grade, I'm sure that there are many factors. I went to my Lilleshall coaching course with a lad called Malcolm Parks. At the time there was nothing to choose between us. Nobody would have dreamed of suggesting that I might make the grade and not Malcolm; it could easily have been the other way round. But it's worked out so that I'm captain of England and he's not even in the professional game. I still see him and he's very happy with his life. We just went different ways.

"I suspect that it didn't mean as much to Malcolm. He was not so single-minded as I was. Determination to succeed is important. And also getting that first start. Once on the staff at Middlesex there were so many great players around for me to watch and learn from that I would have been foolish if I had wasted the opportunity.

"I've already mentioned Mike Smith and Fred Titmus but there were others like Norman Featherstone and John Murray. I found that these players were, on the outside, a little intimidating. However, they were always ready to help if you asked. I think it's important to strike the right balance. You want to be confident in your own ability but you must still be ready to learn."

Good advice, but Mike was preaching to the converted. When I was transferred from Blackpool to Liverpool at the age of eighteen, the fee was a world record for a teenager. I suppose I could have become very big-headed. Fortunately for me there were a few people around to put me straight. More important than the advice was the fact that the Liverpool dressing room was crammed with good players. Ron Yeats, for example, was captain of his country. There was Roger Hunt, just back from winning a World Cup medal, and Ian St John, one of the greatest footballers ever to wear a Liverpool shirt. I took one look around at the team and had to tell myself, in no uncertain terms: "Em, you've done nowt yet. This is where the hard work starts."

I told Mike my story, and asked if his feelings were the same.

"Middlesex, when I joined them, were not quite the great side they became a few years later under Mike Brearley. It was when I was appointed captain that I had to tell myself that I was starting all over again. Following a successful skipper is very hard. People will tell you that they don't expect you to achieve immediate success and that it will take time for you to establish yourself, but underneath they probably do anticipate you continuing in the winning ways of your predecessor. They're certainly disappointed if you don't. Mike had established winning ways which made things easier for me, but I still had it all to do."

This mention of Gatt's role as skipper of Middlesex was the chance I wanted to raise the vexed question of his England captaincy. There's no doubt in my mind that the captain of the national cricket side has one of the hardest jobs in sport. Being captain at football wasn't easy, but I'm the first to admit that the skipper's job on the football field can be a bit easier than that of his counterpart on the cricket pitch.

Looking at the cricket heroes of my younger days I could name Fred Trueman, John Snow, Ray Illingworth and Brian Close. It doesn't take much to spot common characteristics in that bunch. And I think Mike Gatting could fit happily into that company, cricketers with an aggressive will to win and a healthy disregard for some of the unnecessary niceties of the game. You wouldn't expect "Snowball" or Closey to throw in the towel, and you'd be very surprised to see Fiery Fred or Illy bowing to pressure from on or off the field. Mike was probably hewn from the same rock. His Test career speaks volumes for his gritty ambition, and his dogged self-assertion in the face of umpiring rows and media nonsense during the ill-fated Pakistan tour were greatly applauded by many professionals in sport that I spoke to.

Mike's first Test century didn't arrive until his fifty-fourth England innings, but his ambition was never dampened by his early in-and-out international career. He stuck at the task and eventually got a regular place in the side. The captaincy followed, and then came the controversy.

During my interview with Mike I had no intention at all of raising controversial issues. Enough has been said, and thousands, if not millions, more words will be written on the subjects of player discipline, umpiring standards and the running of the game at international level. But I didn't want the opportunity to pass altogether to ask Mike about the general health of the game. Who is better placed to comment than the England captain?

"I know it's an old grumble, but the media must take some of the blame for what appear to be the modern ills of the game. Take, for example, the business of placing microphones on the pitch. Can you imagine what it would be like if you could hear every word of an international football match?" I shuddered at the thought. The only consolation is that most of the worst offenders speak in Scottish accents and wouldn't be understood anyway.

"That's got to be bad for the game," Mike continued. "Players have been snatching jerseys from umpires, using swear words and generally growling at opponents for as long as the game has been played. In the past we'd all forget the problems at the end of the day and share a drink and a joke. Today we still do the same, but the difference is that we pick up the papers and read of feuds and fights. It gives the game a very bad image, and, as captain, I often take the brunt of the criticism.

"Another problem is the 'winning at all costs' attitude that has crept in. Let's make no mistake about it, I've wanted to win every cricket match I've ever played in. . .and that includes some on the beach with the family. But I can accept defeat and not worry about it. Unfortunately the need to win has meant that some of the humour has been lost, and that's much to the detriment of cricket."

"Do you think that one-day cricket is to blame for that?" I asked.

"One-day cricket did a lot for the game, bringing the crowds back and giving a lot of players a new lease of life. It also coincided with the introduction of overseas players into the English game. That was generally good, although I'm not sorry that they're bringing the limit back down to one this year.

"I don't think there's one single reason for the problems of the game, but the introduction of greater financial incentives has increased the pressures on and off the field. As a captain and a cricket lover, my main concern is for the younger players coming into the game for the first time. They are expected, and here we go back to the problems created by the media again, to succeed very quickly indeed. We all know that you've got to be able to cope with the pressures of professional sport but youngsters need, and deserve, some special consideration. They are the lifeblood of the future so we ought to nurture them a bit, not thrust them into the limelight and then knock them if they don't come up to expectations."

"Talking of the future, Mike, what are your hopes?" I asked Mike this since we had been talking about the future but also because, like so many of the top stars I've interviewed, Mike had achieved almost everything that his particular sport had to offer. What drove him on? His answer was the kind I would expect from a man who, although self-assured and happy to speak his own mind, clearly has a deep love of cricket and puts the interests of the sport before personal ambition.

"My ambitions are mainly for cricket now, rather than for myself. Yes I want to carry on as captain of England and Middlesex. I'm nowhere near the end of my career and it would be nice to be able to think about bowing out when I'm at the top. But in the broader sense I want to see cricket through its current 'crisis'.

"When I joined the professional game it was just on the turn round from a series of moribund years. The County Championship was frankly dull and the Test series, although made exciting by some individual players, never really captured the imagination. One-day cricket, sponsorship and a number of new personalities changed all that. Now, after a period of boom, we seem to have reached a sticky patch. There's too much cricket, in my opinion, and the cracks are beginning to show.. Top players aren't wanting to tour, the public are expected to show an interest in a large number of tournaments, and somehow the news about cricket concentrates on incident and personality, not on results and performances.

"If my contribution has been to help cricket in any way, then that's an ambition fulfilled. As we sit here there are plenty of people who think I've done the game a disservice by arguing with an umpire. My view is that those who created the problem in the first place were being disrespectful to the game, and I couldn't stand by and watch. The whole incident in Pakistan, where a day's play was lost due to squabbling, is now history. But if cricket can learn from its history, and I hope it can, then some good will come out of the incident.

"Perhaps the end result will be a review of umpiring policy around the world. I know that action replays make the game much harder for umpires, and that the men in white coats suffer from media exposure just like the players, but everybody will agree that the situation is not right at the moment. Let's face it, sport is supposed to be, and can be, an international bridge-builder. When it has the opposite effect, it's time for serious thought."

Any man voicing such sentiments deserves a serious audience. Mike's point about sport being a bridge-builder is so important. You won't find a more patriotic person than me, and I believe that sporting competition can bring people together, not force them apart. Mike symbolises some of our more famous national characteristics: he's determined, gritty and never better than when his back is to the wall. So a few pictures of Gatts, with all that he symbolises, sharing a joke and a drink with opponents, would be most welcome. Let's focus on the positive.

Time was running out and I didn't want our chat to finish on the uncertain future of the great game. It's always nice to let someone tell you what really makes them happy, so I asked Mike what were his greatest moments in sport. I should have specified cricket because, before he mentioned any crucial centuries or great victories, he described several goals he scored for Hendon Reserves. Not quite what I had in mind. The most emotional moment appears to have been the time he stood at Wembley in a capacity crowd and watched his brother walk out with Brighton for an FA Cup Final.

"And in cricket?" I eventually asked.

"Mostly firsts, I think. My first Test hundred, my first tour to Australia, and the two occasions when I've been asked to be captain, first of Middlesex and then of England. I was captain for the Bicentenary Test Match at Lord's against the Rest of the World XI. That was a great honour for me. I suppose I could go on since there seem to have been so many highlights. The tour to Australia when we won absolutely everything that was up for grabs – that was a great thrill for me. English cricket needed success, and it was all the more satisfying because we weren't really tipped to do well. Since being captain of Middlesex we've won at least one tournament every year except 1987. It's always nice to be handed a trophy on behalf of your team; it does make all the hard work worthwhile and it gives something back to the backroom staff, the members and spectators."

If Mike had been subdued when we met, I'm happy to say he was fairly cheerful when we parted. It's quite obvious that he's a cricketer who wants to win, and knows how to win. And he's always going to be happiest when doing that – or at least talking about it. Perhaps we should remember that about Mike and about some of our other sporting greats. Give them the stage and they'll provide the entertainment; tangle them up in arguments and incidents and you'll only get bad news. And bad news is currently spoiling a great game.

Sebastian Coe

a man with a mission

Seb Coe is one of the greatest middle-distance runners of all time, and Britain's most prolific world record setter. In 1979 he became the first man in history to hold world records at 800 metres, 1500 metres and the mile at the same time. He won silver and gold medals in the 1980 Olympics at 800 metres and 1500 metres and made a wonderful recovery from illness to retain the 1500 metres title in the 1984 Olympics and to collect a second silver in the 800 metres. He was awarded the MBE in 1982.

*T*he offices of Adam Faith's management company provided the venue for my talk with Sebastian Coe. In many ways it seemed to be an appropriate place to meet. Seb is a man of the modern media world, easily able to project himself. He's charming, good-looking, successful and provides wonderful entertainment. Adam Faith himself would be delighted with the viewing figures that a Seb Coe race can generate.

I suppose there's the temptation to think that, with all these attributes, Sebastian Coe might be a bit of a smooth customer. Nothing is further from the truth, of course. Although he is ever ready to joke and laugh, and happy to use his charm when the situation demands, his eyes burn with sincerity when he's talking about the issues that matter to him. What matters most at the present time is the state of sport in Great Britain, particularly amongst the young.

Seb, in his work with the Sports Council, is the ideal man to champion the cause. Although I have the highest regard for a great number of our athletes, Seb is the one who best represents all the positive virtues and advantages of sport at every level. I say "every level" because Seb, like so many of my "Great Britons", does not limit his interest to Olympic or international sport. He doesn't even restrict his involvement to athletics. He's happy to talk about any sport, although there's one word of warning I ought to give: try to avoid any unkind references to Chelsea Football Club. I know that can be hard, but Seb is very touchy about it.

I suppose Chelsea Football Club, or indeed any football club, may be a symbol of the kind of problem that Seb is tackling. When we think of football today we often think of boardroom struggles, sacked managers, hooliganism, cash crises and even sex scandals. The football itself is left well behind. Athletics, too, has had its share of bad news with the Budd affair, rigged results, drug taking and Olympic boycotts. Not that Seb is out to put the world right at a single stroke, but he believes that we can improve our future by putting effort into developing sport for the young. He talks about the missing million, the number of kids that one would expect to be involved in sport and who have no interest whatsoever. What, exactly, are the roots of the problem was one of the first questions I put to Seb.

"I'm not saying that schools are always at fault, but it's in schools that we've got to start the rehabilitation programme. Under the newly proposed national curriculum, a model for the school year that every school will have to follow, PE is allocated five per cent of the timetable. That means about one period of thirty to forty minutes each week. If it takes ten minutes to get changed at the beginning and end of each session, what hope is there of the kids ever getting their hearbeats up above normal? What chance also is there for kids to experience and enjoy new sports?

"Take the recent strike action in schools, for example," Seb continued. "That meant that there were few or no games going on outside normal hours. School teams were hit and regional competition between schools came to an almost complete standstill.

"I'm not apportioning blame but pointing out that we'll produce a generation of uninterested and unfit children if we're not careful."

What Seb was saying to me was not news. It's been all too obvious for a long time that watching sport seems to be more important than playing sport, and that even watching sport is less popular than it was. Soap opera, computer games and pop music seem to be about the extent of most kids' interests these days. I'm the last one to want to sound like some long-playing record, moaning on about how the young should behave. My own experiences, however, have proved to me what a wonderful thing sport can be. Even my own children, who seem to spend half their lives with personal radios stuck in their ears to drown out Dad's grumbling, will admit that sport has already provided them with good exercise, great fun and some special memories.

So how can we get people to listen to what Seb has to say? I suppose if I knew the answer I'd be doing his job and not mine. But we have got to convince all those concerned with the young that sport, and health, are worth bothering about.

Why I feel so delighted that Seb is involved with the efforts to promote sport is that his upbringing in sport, like mine, was exceptional only because it was so normal.

"I was just like all the other kids I knew," Seb explained. "I was sports mad. I never walked anywhere, I always ran. If I needed to run, I'd sprint. Anything that was round became a football and every distant object was a finishing line. I played any and every sport I could.

"The records will show that I came fourth in the Warwickshire Schools one-hundred yards in 1968. That was when we were living in Stratford. We then moved to Sheffield where, again, I did everything I possibly could. It was our PE teacher, John O'Keefe, who helped me into athletics and encouraged me to join a club, the Hallamshire Harriers. At the time I had no idea that athletics could become a career, of course, but, at about fifteen or so, I did begin to think seriously about it. That was because I started getting knocks at football that prevented me from producing my best in running events. So I tended to give up on most other sports and concentrate on running – although I did compete in both the javelin and high jump at various times for the Harriers. It was mostly cross-country in the winter and everything else in the summer."

"And when did middle-distance start to dominate?"

"As I became better at it, it seemed to choose me rather than me choose

117

it. I do remember not liking sprints. They were always over too quickly. And I didn't have the right build for some of the field events. Probably the turning point was an article I saw in the Sheffield evening paper, the green 'un as it's always been known. They ran an article on me, charting my progress through to competing at national youth level in the 1500 metres. It was nice to be recognised. The article also mentioned the Olympics I would be setting my sights on.

"To tell the truth I had never thought about it until then. The paper had exercised a little journalistic imagination which turned out to be an accurate prediction.

"At the same time I came to the attention of national coaches. This meant a greater degree of opportunity as I was encouraged to attend events and training courses."

"And were your teachers still involved in your coaching?"

"To a degree, but by the time I was sixteen my father was my main guide. He had become interested as I had progressed and had spoken to one or two of the other coaches around the country. Eventually he started reading up, attending courses and working as hard at learning coaching as I was at learning running. It was a good partnership."

"And anyone could do it?" That was the key question. Could Seb's example work for anyone?

"Of course. Clearly not everybody wins gold medals but anyone can start. You then work until you find your own level. And once you've made that start you're always likely to want to do something in the sports line."

I thought of my children again. I'm not going to write here whether they will or won't represent their country at their chosen sports, but I do hope they reach the level at which they get most enjoyment. Importantly they're going to be happier and fitter from playing sport. And they give their old man a thrill too.

If Seb's early life could be a model for any aspiring athlete, his career after leaving school could make great material for a feature film writer. It has all the ingredients of a dramatic spectacular: defeat and disappointment, victory and vindication all set against the dramatic back-cloth of Olympic competition. His comebacks could make *Rocky* films look like seaside variety shows, and his bitter duels with Steve Ovett put *Gunfight at the OK Corral* in the shade. I'm getting carried away – but what a story. The Moscow Olympics seemed to have a script too outrageous to be true. How did Seb remember them, and what was the background to those dramatic few days that stirred the whole athletics world into a frenzy of excitement?

"As I said earlier, it was some while before I started thinking about

Olympic competition. But by the time the 1976 Games came around I was beginning to realise that, if I ever was going to reach an Olympics, it was going to be next time around. I was also beginning to see my heroes come within striking distance.

"My first heroes were all footballers, people like Rodney Marsh and George Best, but I soon started following the achievements of athletes. I particularly admired runners like David Bedford, Alan Pascoe and David Hemery. But since they didn't run in my events I tended to look abroad for my role models. At the time John Walker from New Zealand and Lasse Viren, the flying Finn, were the leaders of the pack. And then came a chap called Steve Ovett!

"Steve did a lot for British middle-distance running by simply winning events and getting in the public eye. I know Steve will laugh if he reads this, but it's true to say that he was an early hero of mine. That we became great rivals is ironic because his achievements spurred me on to compete in his events.

"I remember him winning a 1500 at the World Cup in 1977. The race coincided with *Match of the Day* and I had to turn over to watch it. What I saw made me tremble with excitement. Steve kicked at the bottom bend and cruised past the field with such ease. I know it's an old cliché to say that the others looked as if they were standing still, but that's exactly what it seemed like to me. I think the exciting thing was that I could relate to the victory. I knew I was a little way off achieving that sort of performance but I could feel the sensation of winning such a race in my bones. I knew I had it in me."

I could also remember that race, and the resulting interest in the two events, the 800 metres and the 1500 metres. I think this interest coincided with the appearance of several Britons capable of medal winning performances. And there's also the fact that races of this length make good armchair drama. The time it takes to run an 800 metres, and more particularly a 1500 metres, is ideal for television. You're first introduced to all the principal characters, who then act out an exciting story. The ending is never clear until the last few moments. After the race you've still got the excitement of the victory celebrations and a few words from those involved. If you add to these ingredients the celebrated heroes and villains like Seb Coe, Steve Ovett and Steve Cram, it's no wonder that middle-distance running assumed a prominent place in athletics reporting.

Seb understood why middle-distance, for me, was so popular and added the point that the 800 and 1500 metre events were those in which Britons raced against the rest of the world – with a good chance of winning. There weren't many events for which the same claim could be made.

"There were also very exciting athletes around. For example, at 400 metres Alberto Juantorena, the giant Cuban, was winning everything in sight. It was strongly rumoured that he would be an even better runner at 800 metres. And there were Africans too, in the top flight, such as Filbert Bayi of Tanzania. Runners from another continent always add that little bit extra."

"But when did it start to become Coe versus Ovett?" I asked, for that was the confrontation that really captured the public's imagination.

"In many ways," Seb responded, "the Moscow Olympics were all about Coe versus Ovett. For some commentators at least, nothing much else seemed to matter."

In some ways that was not so surprising because, going into the Games, you had two supreme athletes who were both peaking at the same time. Yes, Steve's challenge for medals was based on more experience than that of his younger rival, but Seb was in such inspired form that few people saw how he could lose a race, especially at 800 metres. The stage was set for two classic encounters; everything associated with the rivalry seemed only to increase the drama.

Seb was the great record breaker – in fact setting eight world records between 1979 and 1981. Steve, however, was the great fighter. No matter how fast the pace, there was nothing Steve relished more than a good race. Seb was the gentleman, courteous, outgoing and relaxed. Steve, while never being ungentlemanly, was more of a loner, more ready to shun critics and fans alike. And, to cap it all, Seb and Steve, through a combination of luck and design, had never competed in races of this importance when they had both been fit enough to make the challenge worthwhile. This really was a showdown.

"I got this feeling of showdown from the moment I entered the Olympic village," Seb confessed. "The first, and perhaps most obvious, thing was the fact that Steve and I, even though we were in the same team, seemed to be roomed as far apart as it was possible to be. Then there were all the questions, always concentrating on Steve and I, never on any of the other runners. I had to work hard to maintain concentration, particularly as there were heats in our events.

"The fact that neither Steve nor I ever said unfair or unkind things about the other, in fact never said anything at all for most of the time, also appeared to make matters worse. In the absence of quotes the papers don't say nothing, they make things up. It suited the media to make us the focal point of the Olympics. As we've said already, it was great drama. I suppose you can't blame them for hyping it up a bit."

"And how was the rivalry on a personal level?" I asked.

"I suppose it would be predictable if I said that we were actually great friends. The truth is, however, that I hardly knew the man. Our longest conversations until 1980 were probably handshakes and grunts of good wishes at the start of a race. I'm grateful to Steve that he adopted the same 'don't tell' attitude as me. This made life a lot easier so when I saw 'I'll get you Seb!' or 'Why I'm going to whip Seb' types of headline, I knew it was all a load of paper talk. Steve had said nothing of the sort."

"And what about the races themselves?" I knew I had to ask this because I wanted to know how Seb felt during the first of the two finals, the 800 metres. I can recall shouting at my own television set during that famous race, telling Seb, from 2000 miles away, that there was no way he could win the race, positioned, as he was, at the back of the field. I can hear myself now shouting 'get going, get involved' and wondering if he was unwell or something. All that emotion, and I don't think I even had a bet on it. You couldn't have got decent odds on a Coe victory anyway.

"It was nerves during that 800 metres. All those things you were shouting at your TV – I was saying to myself. But I just couldn't do it. After a bad start, coupled with nerves that seemed to take a grip of me, I just couldn't get into a winning position. Steve did me and I had to settle for the silver."

"How big a blow was that to your confidence?"

"Big enough. But again, reading about it made things seem worse. After all, I'd only lost a race, it wasn't the end of the world. I suppose the worst thing was knowing that I'd run a bad race in an event I knew that I could have won. Unfortunately I picked the Olympic final for my disaster of the season. Why couldn't it have been the inter-counties championships at Leicester?

"Of course, at the time, I had the 1500 metres final still to look forward to, although most pundits were already awarding that to Steve. The 1500 metres is the 'blue ribbon' event of the games. From my point of view it offered a chance to regain some pride. It was also a race in which I could afford a lap in which to settle down and conquer any nerves. If you get into your stride you can float a little in the race – unlike the 800 metres which is solid racing." In Moscow, as we all know, it came right for Seb.

His gold medal triumph in the 1500 metres not only proved the critics wrong, but gave the expectant public as much drama and excitement as they could possible have wished for. Four years after thinking "next time will be the one for me", Seb stood on the rostrum, gold medal around his neck and a silver in his pocket.

If Moscow represented the dramatic climax to a personal duel, Los Angeles in 1984 was the re-assertion of Coe's domination of the 800 and 1500 metres events. He exactly duplicated his medal haul, becoming the first man to defend the "blue ribbon" when he took a brilliant gold in the 1500 metres.

And for those who thought that the rivalry between Coe and Ovett reached the stage of personal animosity, you only have to listen to Seb's description of events on the track in Los Angeles. These are the heartfelt comments of a friend and fellow athlete:

"I went over to Steve, who was kneeling down, and patted him on the back. I remember seeing that he was panting particularly hard and so said to him that the trouble was that he and I were just getting too old for all this. I then turned away. The next thing I saw was a man running towards Steve who was now looking quite drawn. A stretcher was brought over and he was given some oxygen. I was surprised at this, but it was nothing out of the ordinary.

"In the tunnel, however, things got a lot worse. Steve had been left to recover for a moment and I noticed just how white he was. I called for medical help quickly and, thankfully, he was in an ambulance within minutes. Steve was in real trouble in that tunnel. I'm not exaggerating when I say I was seriously worried for a few minutes; I don't think I've seen other competitors quite so bad. I certainly don't want to again."

I remembered at Liverpool there was always the problem of whether to confess to The Boss if you didn't feel one hundred per cent. If you played badly because of injury or illness, you could be dropped next time round. If you let somebody else have your place, you might never get it back again. The choice, of course, wasn't always yours. When Shanks was manager he didn't take illness that seriously.

I asked Seb if athletes faced similar dilemmas.

"The problem in events like the 800 and 1500 metres is that there are so many guys waiting to take your place. If I'm fit I reckon I can do any of them. Take as little as two or three per cent away from me, and they're snapping at my heels. I never know what to do; sometimes you can convince yourself you're OK and other times you know you just can't race.

"Steve knew he was wrong to have run in Los Angeles, but there was a lot of pressure on him to compete. Unfortunately we could have had a British one, two and three in the 1500 metres if he had been fit. But that's history."

"And talking of history, are there things you regret?"

"None. That may seem hard to believe, but I've enjoyed it all – and that means the downs and the ups.

"Let's face it, if you wanted to show a film of all the things not to do in an 800 metres race, you'd show my Moscow effort. But I still wouldn't change it. I won my first international 800 metres title in Stuttgart in 1986 at the age of thirty; that was a great thrill and made up for many disappointments before. Perhaps I'll be the first thirty-two-year-old to win an Olympic gold in the event in Seoul. That's the kind of thing that keeps you going. There's no point at all in regretting the past."

I knew exactly what Seb meant. You must not dwell on the past in a negative way; enjoy what's gone, whether it's good or bad. And also keep looking forward. I certainly found that some aspects of my game improved as I progressed in the game. Training actually got easier. And I also found I was able to relax and enjoy it more. The pressure was off.

"My philosophy," Seb explained, "is that 1980 was for experience, 1984 for medals and 1988 is for enjoyment."

What more can I say than "good luck to him"? That "good luck" is not only for his fight to win medals, but also for his campaign against drugs in sport and his struggle to get a better deal for youngsters. And if Seb's past form is anything to go by, he won't need much luck and we'll all be enjoying more medal winning performances from the man, and also a better future for sport in Britain. I think Seb would settle for the second achievement, but would greatly enjoy the first.

Nora Perry

the lesson of experience

Nora Perry is one of England's greatest badminton doubles players of all time. She started playing at the age of twelve and, with Gillian Gilks, dominated women's doubles for a full decade. She has won the All-England Championship seven times, is a triple Commonwealth gold medallist and twice world champion. In the 1985 World Championships she won the silver medal. She has ninety caps for England, and in 1984 was awarded the MBE. She has cut down on international commitments recently to spend more time with her family.

*W*hat does it take to reach the top in international sport? Determination, natural ability, a strong sense of ambition and the willingness to make sacrifices will certainly be on any list of requirements. But what does it take to reach the top if you're British, a woman and playing in a minority sport? I'm afraid to say that it requires a lot more than the list I've already given.

Nora Perry needed many things that her international opponents never dreamed of. For a start she needed a job to give her the money to compete. Her Far Eastern rivals in particular would have found this quite incredible. Then she needed extreme single-mindedness and self-confidence to go out and beat the world when the British press and public seemed to be totally indifferent to her achievements. And, most of all, and perhaps most amazing of all, she needed a very thick skin to ward off the criticisms and accusations from her sport's own controlling body – the very people who were supposed to be helping her in her quest for honours.

And also, I nearly forgot, there was the arrival of baby Gemma in the middle of a campaign to win the World Mixed Doubles Championship that didn't exactly help matters. . .although you won't find Nora complaining about that event!

To be truthful, you won't find Nora complaining about much in life. When she's in full flow about the sport she loves, however, you can't help but detect a sense of disappointment about the way she has been treated. One's attitude to the problems she's faced does depend on the way we think we ought to tackle sport in this country. I'm not going to comment on that, for the moment, but let Nora tell her story. The way she started in badminton typifies the British approach. This is Nora talking about badminton, but there are many similarities between her and my other "Great Britons".

"I started when I was about twelve or so at secondary school in Essex. I used to enjoy playing tennis but the courts were often unplayable because of the weather. When that was the case I'd go in and watch the other pupils play badminton. We had one court marked out in the assembly hall. However, only fourth- and fifth-year kids played so I'd have to watch. Sometimes, though, the teacher would ask me to play to make up the numbers. I was hopeless. However, I stuck at it just because I loved sport and there was nothing else to do when it was raining. Eventually I got better and the teacher asked me to play a bit more often. It grew from there.

"I don't think there are so many schools playing badminton today. It's often something kids just do as an option in the later years. They probably go to a sports centre and have a few games before getting a job and forgetting about sport altogether.

"Anyway, my teacher, Mr Tinworth, who's still at the school in Corringham, encouraged me to go further. I played for the county schools' team at both badminton and tennis. My parents knew I was good and they helped me a lot too. In fact they even discussed with me the prospect of taking up sport seriously when I left school. My father said that I ought to concentrate on tennis because there was plenty of money in the sport. I listened to him and packed up tennis and concentrated on badminton. I guess you're like that when you're sixteen!"

"Deciding to play badminton meant that you'd have to look for a full-time job, presumably. Looking back do you now wish that you could have gone straight into sport?" I asked Nora this, wondering if she felt in any way jealous of the money that is now becoming available for a few, and only a few, children to go into full-time sport on leaving school.

"No. I had two parts to my life. I had my work with Lloyd's Bank, who were terrific employers, and I had my badminton. That's not to say it wasn't hard. Of course all my holiday went on playing badminton and then I'd get extra time off too. It was sometimes difficult to make a sudden switch from sport to work. For example, I remember the first time I won the All-England Ladies Doubles in 1976. I played about twenty matches I think, on Friday evening, all day Saturday and all day Sunday. Winning the All-England, which was then like winning the world championship, was a dream come true for me. I felt wonderful. Going back to work on Monday morning was a hard adjustment to make.

"I had always taken the view that having a job meant I got the best of both worlds. You have to think like that, otherwise you'll resent work and your ill-feeling will rub off on your game. Another good thing was that I spent years budgeting to enable me to travel and compete. When some cash started entering the sport, it came as a real bonus for me. I appreciated it so much more than some players who have been reared on sponsorship and appearance money.

"I can still remember winning four pounds at the age of eighteen when Maggie Beck and I beat the favourites 17–15 in the third game for the Surrey Championships at the Wimbledon Squash and Badminton Club. I felt fantastic.

"Today, many of the youngsters think that they're going to become millionaires simply by being average at their sport. That's a bad thing. They've got to realise that there's a lot of hard work involved. I think the desire to win has got to come first. The idea of fame and money might be in one's mind, but it can't be allowed to dominate."

I knew exactly what Nora was driving at by these comments. It takes me back to my introduction to this chapter. Is it easy being a young British hopeful in a sport like tennis or badminton? On the one hand, there is considerable disquiet about the way we tend to neglect our children's development. In sports like tennis and badminton the facilities are poor, the coaching structure is often outmoded, there's a lack of coordination between schools, and the clubs and some of the ruling bodies seem to be totally out of touch with what is going on. On the other hand, there's also a lot of anxiety about the direction in which we might move if we adopt the model of the United States or Eastern Europe. Do we want our kids plucked out of normal school at a very young age and pushed to their limits in training and competition?

Nora's experience suggests that the British approach works. She made her name in badminton in spite of the many disincentives and disadvantages. Perhaps things would have been different for her if everything had been laid on a plate. I asked about this.

"It's a very difficult one. I know that many of my colleagues in badminton have given a lot of thought to it. There's nothing wrong with having to work your way to the top; but there's nothing wrong either in having a bit of help on the way.

"I often look at the players we come up against from the Far East. Indonesians, Malayans, Koreans and, in particular, the Chinese take badminton very seriously. I've played in front of a crowd of almost twenty thousand before now. They're fanatical in their support of the game. This can mean extra pressure on the players though. One Chinese girl I recall in particular was trained from the age of about six or seven. She had been chosen as a likely future champion and sent to a special school. We were told that, at the schools, they spent about five hours a day practising. At fourteen she was on the fringes of the Chinese team. At eighteen she was world class. She's retired now and she's only twenty-three. I think that's criminal. She's been burnt out and she's fed up with the game. She's nothing left to give to it, and there's nothing more for her to gain from it. That's very sad. It is a game after all.

"I'm thirty-two and I've been playing seriously from about the age of eighteen. That's fourteen years, and now I'm beginning to cut down on my competition and tournament play. This Chinese girl spent seventeen years playing the game seriously so perhaps it's no wonder that she, too, is ready to give it a break. The unfortunate thing is that she started so young and has already had enough. The years I've spent in the game have been great for me; I've enjoyed them and have learned an awful lot. This poor girl has given up her childhood to badminton. That, to me, is a waste."

I listened to Nora with interest. There's no doubt that the point she is making is terribly important. We must not underestimate what it entails to devote yourself to the pursuit of sporting excellence. Kids, if pushed too hard, can suffer badly. But are we right to decide that a child should not have the opportunity to develop a particular talent? My father was a professional sportsman, playing rugby league football. I know how delighted he was to see me achieve my ambition to play professional soccer. It gave him no end of satisfaction to see me running out with a Liverpool or England shirt on. He did everything he could to encourage me but, in those days, that wasn't much. He'd make sure I had proper kit and the bus fare to get to games. He would also talk to people on my behalf and try to push my name forward. But that was about the long and short of it. Supporting me in my sporting ambitions didn't entail sending me away to soccer school or selling the family home to pay for trips abroad or special coaching. I wonder how he would have reacted if things had been different. I think I'm grateful that it never came to that. I hope, also, that my own family can be encouraged without the need to go to such extremes.

Of course, that is the acid test. How do you feel when it's your own family? I put this to Nora.

"Would you allow Gemma to go to a special school for sport if you thought it was the best way, or only way, of her enjoying the sort of success that you have achieved?" was the way I put it to her. Her answer was pretty blunt.

"Absolutely not. I hope Gemma will get as much from sport as I did. But I really want her to play a range of sports, at least until she's in her teens. The main trouble with forcing kids is that they have to concentrate on one thing. To my mind they end up bored and stale and, in some extreme cases, physically affected too."

"So what is the answer? Are we always going to be doing too much or too little?" I felt that Nora had hit upon the contradiction that exists in British sports. We want to be the top but we shy away from the methods needed to achieve that ambition.

"I don't know," Nora replied candidly, "but there must be a middle way. Half the trouble is that we don't seem to be looking for it in a co-ordinated way. Many of the players don't have a lot of confidence in the English Badminton Association."

Some time before my interview with Nora she had been involved in a famous "player-power" incident where the top English players had been at odds with the ruling body and, in particular, the newly appointed badminton supremo Jake Downey. Nora had much to say about that at the time and, as one of the sport's most successful and forthright stars, she was often depicted as the ring-leader. One of the main points of contention was that Downey was trying to impose his methods on the players too strongly, not allowing them to decide their own programmes of training and competing. Nora felt strongly about this at the time, and it obviously still rankled with her.

"The whole Jake Downey thing sums up what I mean. I know Jake, and can still sit down and share a drink and a laugh with him. We're old friends. But at the time his attitude, telling us how long we ought to leave to prepare for our Far Eastern tournaments, was wrong. Apart from the fact that he was physiologically inaccurate, he should have allowed seasoned players to decide for themselves. I'd been there, winning tournaments throughout the world, and knew what I needed to do in order to be properly prepared. I didn't need Jake telling me. There's a world of difference between supporting somebody and trying to dominate them."

One of Nora's main complaints about the whole affair was that the controversy was one of the few times the press seemed really interested in the sport. Apparently her 'phone never stopped ringing when the drama was at its height. I can remember the times with Liverpool when we'd lose two or three games in a spell and the press would suddenly decide there was a crisis going on. Things did get blown up out of all proportion. Anyway, I decided that I wouldn't question her about the incidents; she'd probably said enough about the events to last a lifetime. There was, however, one more point that Nora wanted to make. It related to the Downey affair but really concerned the discussion we were having earlier about the preparation of youngsters in the sport.

"I've always regretted that I've not been asked to help others more in preparing for major championships, particularly those abroad. Part of Jake's problem was that, although he was an excellent coach and a very experienced writer on the game, he hadn't done that much in terms of major successes. Take playing in some of the Far East tournaments, for example.

"I've mentioned before the size of the crowd. Knowing that doesn't prepare for the fact that they're right up to the very edges of the court area. They whistle and shout, jeer you when you make a mistake and give unashamed and fearsome support to their local stars. For example, in 1980 in Jakarta, I reached the finals of both the ladies' and mixed doubles in the World Championships. One match was to follow the other.

"The crowd was around seventeen thousand, and with two local girls in the ladies' final, was baying for victory. I was playing with Jane Webster, who had never experienced such a scene before. We walked on court to the sound of booing – quite some welcome. Jane, or 'Sparky' as I call her, and I couldn't hear ourselves think let alone talk to one another. I actually warmed to the situation. It made me more determined. However, from her first few shots I could see that Jane was having trouble in settling. Fortunately I was able to pull a couple of winners out of the fire and, by constantly encouraging and bullying Jane, she got into her stride. Once we were playing to our best there was no stopping us and we won the gold. It was a fantastic sensation. The crowd, in the end, were marvellous too. They cheered us when we finally won, showing true acknowledgement of just how hard it had been for us.

"After that final I had to go back and try to prepare mentally for my next final, this time playing with Mike Tredgett. I felt a bit envious of Jane, able to go out and celebrate immediately. I didn't feel too bad as I walked on court, however, but I sensed that Mike was a little uneasy. I think he'll agree with me when I say that he froze and we lost a match we might have won. I couldn't do the same with Mike as I had with Jane because mixed doubles is very different from ladies' doubles. In mixed you've got the man behind you all the time, and he's making most of the play. My favourite ploy is to tap my partner on the bottom to encourage them, not easy when they're standing behind you all the time!

"My point is that being prepared for such matches as those is half the battle. I feel I could help other players a lot with my experience. Unfortunately there doesn't seem to be a lot of room for that kind of help. The top coaches are trained as coaches; they have their qualifications and have studied the game in depth. Not nearly enough of them have been there and done it. Experience is not given the credit it deserves."

As I listened to Nora I thought about the problems of playing in a doubles partnership. In a team game like football there's likely to be one player who has a bad game. This can normally be carried, although it's not to be encouraged. I've sometimes surprised people by my attitude to team sport. A point I learned from Bill Shankly is that a team is as good as its weakest player. I've said in interviews before now that I'd get pretty angry if I was playing with somebody like Glenn Hoddle who drifted in and out of game. I'm not singling Glenn out here, but using him as an example. The point is that the other players in the team are playing for *my* wages. Therefore I expect one hundred per cent every match – from everybody.

In Nora's sport you've only one other person to worry about, but what if that person has an off day or didn't, in your mind, give total effort? What about personalities too, if you fell out with your partner?

"All these things happen, but in general partners get on well together. I suppose partnerships are a bit like marriages. Sometimes players with opposite characters get on better; sometimes a partnership is made up of two very similar people.

"I've had some very well-publicised changes of partner. In ladies' doubles I enjoyed a most successful few seasons with Gillian Gilks. She was a wonderful player and we shared some great times. Then there was a problem over coaching and she and I went our separate ways. I teamed up with Jane Webster and it gave me an extra boost to have to prove myself all over again. That World Championship I mentioned earlier was only the second or third serious competition I'd played with Jane. Had I been still with Gill we would have been seeded number one; I think Jane and I were third or fourth seeds."

Nora didn't say that her enforced change in ladies' doubles set her thinking, but she later left Mike Tredgett in what was a more unlikely move.

"I really decided that Mike and I couldn't go on together. We'd played together for a good number of years and won a lot of the big events. We were the major European and Commonwealth pairing for a long time. There came a point, however, where we stopped improving and started to play automatically. What was more worrying was that people stopped being frightened of us and we lost a lot of matches we should have won.

"I didn't just ditch Mike but put it to him that I wanted to make a major assault on the World Mixed Doubles and felt that I ought to change partner. I said I thought we were getting stale and that he couldn't give me the commitment my ambitions demanded. He was, at the time, involved with a building firm. He could look at his diary and tell me which weekends and weeks he would be available – and which he would be working. I needed somebody to give me more than that; I needed almost total commitment. Thomas Kihlstrom was the man who was able to give me the time, although he had two children, and so, on the couple of occasions we got together for practice, I had to fly out to Sweden so he could stay with his family."

Two thoughts immediately sprang to mind. The first concerned the new partner. Why choose a Swede?

"I didn't feel disloyal or unpatriotic. He was the best for me, and Thomas obviously thought I was best for him. The selectors could pair me up with whom they thought best if I was to play for the England team. That was their problem, mine was trying to win the World Mixed Doubles."

"And Thomas's family commitments? Did it affect the way you thought about having children?" I remember seeing Gillian featured in a magazine article, explaining how she tried to combine being a mum with reaching the top in international sport.

"Joe and I planned our family and Gemma came along pretty much when we wanted. I suppose I may have given the matter more thought when I saw other players with children but I think that Joe and I knew what we wanted. I was keen to have a baby when I did so I could still play for a few more seasons when Gemma was young. I thought it would be easier to travel, and I wouldn't mind leaving her so much. That's exactly how it's worked out. I hate leaving Gemma now, and I'm a mother first and badminton player second. It wasn't always like that.

"I entered the whole thing with a very positive attitude and happily things worked out well. I was playing squash until I was eight months, and back in training only three weeks after Gemma was born. I had a number of stitches, though, and that took longer to sort out than I'd imagined." At this point I had to change the subject. Just thinking about the birth of my own children, events I did not witness personally, makes me go faint.

"Tell me Nora," I asked, "what was your greatest moment?" I hoped she wasn't going to describe the birth in detail.

"Very hard to say. I think firsts are always memorable. Looking back, however, I sometimes think that the award of the MBE was the best. I wasn't expecting it at all. I 'phoned round my family and friends when I got the letter and they all seemed to think it was obvious, but I was truly quite shocked.

"The actual day of the presentation was marvellous. I don't know that I was a particular Royal Family fan before, but now I am. The Queen was simply wonderful. She was perfect, as, indeed, was the whole day. The award was saying that my efforts and contribution to the sport were worth something. I was very pleased."

Time was running out but I wanted to ask Nora just a couple of questions about her sport, not a game I'd ever played much. The first concerned the ingredients that go to make up the ideal player.

"I don't think that there's a simple answer to that, but I can tell you what most of the players have got in common. That is they are naturally good at several sports. I think it's because you need both hand–eye co-ordination and natural athletic ability. If you've got both of those you can do all sorts of sports. Take Steve Badderley, for example, our top man at the moment. He's excellent at swimming, tennis and squash – apart from being pretty useful at badminton. As I said before, I think I could have achieved a reasonable standard at tennis, and I play club squash too. I used to do well at cross-country running, but I thought it was making me heavy-legged so I gave up."

My next question, and last, concerned the ingredient that Nora Perry had that so many of her opponents obviously lacked. What precisely was it that drove her on, often against heavy odds, to achieve her world standing in badminton?

"That's actually an easy question to answer because I've thought about it before. The simple answer is – I hate losing. I hate losing at anything, but badminton most of all."

Now in partial retirement, the badminton world is getting some respite from Nora's dread of defeat. Listening to her tell her story I'm delighted that we've got a British champion that we can salute with pride. I know that she would like nothing more than to be considered a good ambassador for her country. But I also think that Nora might like the officials and commentators on the game to draw some lessons from her experiences so that she can leave the game of badminton in a better and healthier state than when she entered it. We surely owe her that.

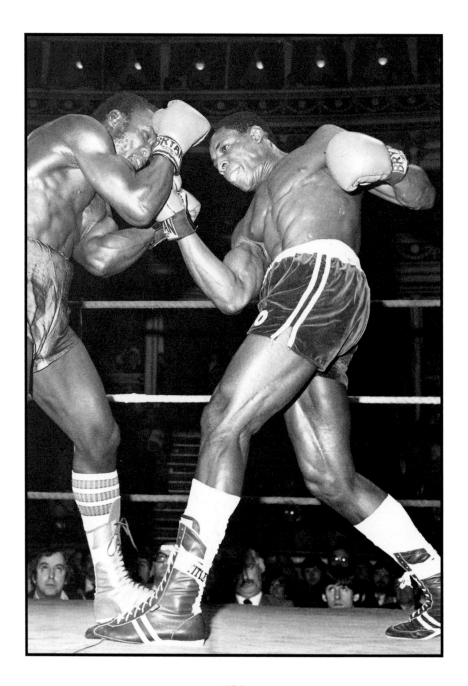

Frank Bruno

Terry's boy

Britain's number one heavyweight boxer, as an amateur Bruno won the ABA Heavyweight title. After turning professional in 1982, at the age of twenty, he took only three years to win the European Heavyweight title, a title which he relinquished undefeated in order to attempt to become the first British boxer this century to win a World Heavyweight title. His dream was shattered by defeat at the hands of Tim Witherspoon in July 1986 – a defeat which does not seem to have deterred him as he seeks to take on reigning World Champion, Mike Tyson.

A little while ago my children were asked to be on a television game show called *Whose Baby?* Children with a famous parent are quizzed by a celebrity panel; the object of the game is for the panel to try to discover who the famous parent is. Since one of my children is called Emlyn I thought it might not be too difficult. However, the panel struggled a bit before deciding that they knew only one ex-England football captain who appeared regularly on *A Question of Sport*.

I shouldn't have scoffed at them because at the end of the programme the producer asked me if I'd like to be a panellist one week. I agreed, but with a little anxiety. I need not have worried. The first child was easily guessed by one of my team, and then the second guest was introduced. This time it was a mother and we had to find out the name of her famous son. Well, from the minute she walked on I knew the answer, and I couldn't stop laughing. The mother just had to be – there could be no possible mistake – Mrs Bruno. She walked like Frank, looked like Frank, and when she opened her mouth I was convinced she was going to ask where Harry was. It was a hoot, and I think she enjoyed it as much as the audience and the other panellists.

That Frank Bruno is so universally popular, and that his name is associated with all the good things in sport, is a credit to the man. It wasn't always the case. There were many days when Frank must have thought that nobody outside the East End of London would ever get to hear of him. But today, if you mention his name, people smile with pleasure. He is everybody's favourite son, and his ambitions are now those of the nation.

To interview Frank meant going back to his roots in more ways than one. For, not only did I want to hear about his early days, but we'd decided to meet at the gym he uses, above the Royal Oak public house in Canning Town, not far from where he was born. It was about those early days, in and around the East End, that I asked Frank first.

"To say I was like any other kid is not quite true," announced Frank in his deep, resonant voice. "I was always large-boned and normally quite a bit bigger than other boys of my age. We'd do the normal things, scrapping in the streets, charging about up to no good. But there was nothing unpleasant in what we did, just a bunch of kids really."

"So when did you start boxing?"

"When I was about eight. It was because I was big that I got started and I quickly learned how to use my fists. I could beat all the kids in my age range but, every so often, I'd get moved up a notch. That meant you'd be the youngest in your section and I used to take some beatings then.

"Perhaps I got a bit too big for my boots because I was sent away to boarding school when I was about eleven or twelve. Apparently I was

138

difficult to control! Anyway I carried on with my boxing and got in the Young England boxing team. Things were going well, but I was not very settled in life. I wasn't sure what I wanted to do."

"How did you move into professional boxing?"

"That came much later. I had to make it in the amateur ranks first. I remember thinking that boxing might represent a good opportunity for me, and that I ought to try to make the most of it. I looked around and saw the prospects for me as being pretty slim. I could work in a supermarket or warehouse or I might even get some minor office job. But these things weren't going to satisfy my needs. I saw golfers and tennis players earning plenty of dosh, even after they'd given their bit to Mrs Thatch. I wondered where mine was coming from. I couldn't make it in soccer so boxing looked the most likely bet for me. I just wanted to give it a go."

As Frank spoke I looked out over the gym. There were half a dozen guys, of various weights, going through their paces. A couple sweating and sparring in the ring, another pair working out on the bags and others skipping and mirror-boxing. Was I looking at a future world champion? I couldn't tell; nobody could. Terry Lawless, Frank's manager and the gym's proprietor, might have a better idea than most. But even he would be the first to admit that there's a lot that can go wrong between stepping out on one's career and reaching the moment when you get to the top. That's why Frank's decision was a gamble, and happily one that paid off. But it could have ended in disaster and Frank would have found himself looking at the warehouse or supermarket once more, only this time with the stigma of being a failed boxer.

I wondered if there was one thing that, for Frank, marked the transition from gifted amateur to hard-nosed professional.

"Nothing in particular. I joined Wandsworth Club and met a guy called Gary Leverton. His father, John, and Gary helped me a lot. I got on, left school and did a number of jobs. I was a bouncer, worked on a building site and even did some metal polishing. But still boxing held out the only realistic hope for me. Then, when I was eighteen, I won the ABA Heavyweight Championship.

"A guy with a cigar and a Rolls Royce came to see me. He brought his cheque book with him too. I suddenly thought I'd made it. Turning professional would be the end of my worries. It didn't work out like that."

"This was Terry?" I asked.

"No. It was Terry who had to buy up my contract from this guy. I left it to him to sort out the money side of things. I should have known better. You don't get nothing in this life without working for it. It was Terry who explained to me that turning professional wasn't the end; it was the start.

The work really began once I was under Terry's wing. The first problem was failing a health test with the British Board of Boxing Control. I had an eyesight problem in one eye. Eventually I had to go to Columbia to have an operation and get it sorted out.

"Then the learning began. There was just so much that I didn't know. I had to go back to school, only this time the teachers seemed to believe in me."

"Were there any people who helped you especially?" I asked.

"There wouldn't be room in your pad if I told you all their names." Frank took hold of my notes and shook them in the air as he spoke. As I reclaimed them I realised that neither my pad, nor the pocket tape recorder I used for some interviews, could capture the essence of the man who sat beside me. He was simply larger than life. For a start he's a born story teller. I didn't need to interview him; I had merely started him off and now, from time to time, I just had to point his story in the direction I wanted it to go. I didn't need to think of superlatives to describe him; superlatives wouldn't be enough. All I had to do was listen, note down what he said, and let the tale unfold. Frank was more than capable of providing the entertainment.

"Of course," Frank was off again, getting more animated as he went along. "It wasn't just the fight game that I needed to learn. I was growing up in every way. As an amateur I'd been to Ireland and Germany, fighting with Young England. That was great and broadened my perspective on life. Terry's management helped me meet more people and go more places. I found myself eating out, something I'd not done much of before, and moving in circles that I'd normally not mix in."

I told Frank that I was eighteen before I had a meal in a restaurant. In fact I was going to tell him something else too, but I wasn't quick enough.

"Meals are the hardest thing, you know what I mean?" Frank threw in one of his favourite phrases. In fact I was to hear the words another fifty or sixty times. If you want to get the flavour of Frank's speech, just add "you know what I mean?" to the end of everything he says. You'll soon find what a useful phrase it is, you know what I mean?

But there's no time to pause right now. Frank was keen to explain the Bruno method of eating out. "It's easy. I just wait to see what the other people do. If they start with the bread roll, I start with the bread roll; if they use a spoon, I use a spoon; if they pick their nose, Frank Bruno picks his nose. Magic. Sometimes I'm the main guest and they're waiting for me; the soup can get very cold then.

"All those extra bits are fun. And I enjoy the training too. But going into the ring has never been fun. That's really hard work, make no mistake about it.

"But it's in the ring where the business is done. And it was in choosing my opponents that Terry really helped me. I had success when my confidence needed boosting, and I had hard fights when I needed to learn a lesson. Terry also helped me keep my feet on the ground when the media started to take an interest."

In boxing, I thought, there's only one goal for the dedicated professional. That's got to be the championship of the world. There must be a moment in every boxer's life when he knows, in himself, that he may have what it takes. Many boxers, of course, never get that far; the brave ones are those that can admit that fact to themselves.

Then there are those boxers that become their managers' great hope. Everybody in the game knows that they're not going to get that crown; the managers are indulging in dangerous hype. But unfortunately boxing is all about contenders and claims, and the outright no-hopers, whose challenges are built of nothing more than brave words and a few prayers, will always be with us.

Then there are the Frank Brunos of this world: men who do have that realistic hope. For Frank there must have been a moment, perhaps prompted by a newspaper headline or a whispered ringside comment, when he first thought he could go all the way. I asked him about this.

"Not really, Em. I guess the idea just grew slowly. However, when people did start talking about it I suddenly became much more nervous. I tensed up. One day I'd be running fifteen miles, no problem, and the next my legs seemed to go stiff."

"Apart from the nerves, were there any other problems? Did all the attention start to get to you?"

"As I said before, Terry was good for me and helped me keep my feet on the floor. But I had that in me from the start. Some blokes, like Lloyd Honeyghan, for example, seem to go a bit wild. I was never like that. I've said it before in interviews: I don't want to be famous, I just want some more money."

Not want to be famous. You have got to laugh at that. For whether he tried hard or not, Frank Bruno has become one of the biggest media successes in recent years. His popularity goes far beyond sport; he's the ideal chat show guest, quiz show celebrity and television panellist. Much to his credit he's done plenty of charity work on television, his Romeo and Juliet sketch with Lenny Henry being one of the most famous of its kind. I'm also pleased to say he's joined me on A Question of Sport and, the less said about this the better, on Spitting Image. Whatever it is that delights the British public, he's got it to excess.

The most important factor in promoting a personality today is the power of television. Whether or not Frank Bruno wants to be famous, his manager, Terry Lawless, has got to be able to sell his fights. Selling ringside seats and making a few bob on programme and souvenir sales wouldn't pay for the cost of the catering these days. It's television rights, sold to the UK and across the world, that make the money. And Frank's command of the medium, intentional or not, is what has made him his pile. As he said, he's got some of the money he wants but he wants some more. Television will probably ensure that his wishes come true.

The question I wanted to put to Frank was whether he was a natural performer or whether he's been learning the art of acting as quickly as he's been learning to box.

"It's all natural, Em. I just go out there and try to be myself. I'd be no good if I tried to learn any lines or anything like that."

Could this be true? I recalled the famous moment at the end of the Bugner fight, when Frank asked Jim Rosenthal from ITV where Harry Carpenter was. The BBC was not covering the fight as ITV had exclusive rights. Was that a genuine off-the-cuff comment? I think it was, but I wasn't going to put Frank on the line and ask him. Who cares anyway, it was great television and undoubtedly one of the quotes of the year. "Where's Harry?" now ranks alongside some of Frank's other catch-phrases. You really don't need a *Spitting Image* take-off; the real thing is better any day of the week.

Television and Frank go together and, as David Coleman suggested, Bruno may eventually fill the place of Henry Cooper – an ex-boxer with charm, intelligence, natural wit and a gift of the gab. But that's all in the future. You've got to be somebody first before television takes you up, and Frank Bruno is the number one British contender for the heavyweight championship of the world. Frank, all being well, is due to challenge for Tyson's crown in September. By the time you read this, that may be history. With luck, you'll be reading about Frank Bruno, the heavyweight champion of the world. The best I can do is to wish Frank luck and look at the events that led up to his brave challenge.

As Frank himself explained, he benefited from a carefully managed schedule of training and fights. Naturally the press started writing about his chances in world terms and this culminated in a much-publicised fight with James "Bonecrusher" Smith. I asked Frank about this.

"That was me being too young and too inexperienced. I had him for nine rounds. If I was in that position today I'd do everything I could to avoid even meeting the bloke again until the end of the fight. I'd pretend my bootlace had come undone, I'd slip over and take counts of eight. . .anything but expose myself to a punch. Unfortunately I was still trying to prove to people what a brave boy I was. I was proud too. I wanted to go out and fight and finish him off. I see now that it was wrong, but at the time I couldn't do anything else. That was me boxing from my heart, not my brain. I'm more cool now. I don't do that sort of thing."

"And what about the Tim Witherspoon fight, where you had your first crack at a world crown? I was right behind you but I must say I didn't think you were ready."

"Maybe. It was a problem. We had a chance and had to gamble. I didn't know when the next chance would come along and there's no doubt that I was good enough to beat Witherspoon. It's just that things didn't work out on the night.

"I've got youth on my side so knew that if I did lose there might be a later chance. But I didn't go in there expecting to get beat."

To my mind the result was right and Frank didn't really look ready to challenge and defend – and defending the championship is the mark of greatness. And at the time Witherspoon only held one version of the championship. Let's make no mistake about it, everybody knew that Tyson would be the man to beat. Now that Tyson has got all three versions wrapped up, Frank really is in line for the undisputed championship. If he beats mighty Mike Tyson there will not be a voice anywhere in the world who would dare diminish his performance.

Frank clearly feels stronger in himself now, more confident about what he wants in and out of the ring. Here's how he put it:

"They did me no harm at all. Those defeats put hairs on my chest." I don't think anybody was going to suggest that he didn't have hairs on his chest before, but "we know what you mean" Frank.

In one sense Frank's career is about waiting for the big one. But there have been some great nights in his career; we only seem to have talked about the defeats so far. I asked him what was his most memorable moment. The answer came back in a flash.

"Beating Joe Bugner. If I'd lost that one I'd have left the country. I wouldn't have been able to look anyone in the face again. I knew I could win, and knew I had to win. But I was a bit scared."

"Scared of what?" I asked. "It's obvious that you were the better, fitter and stronger boxer."

"Yes, but he had all the experience. And he used it in the fight too. He did everything he could to stop me. I really had to be alert. I'd put up with his comments beforehand and was very pleased to see the back of him."

"People looked out for your punch that night, and I think people hope that it will be your punch that works on Tyson. How do you think about your game, though, is it all down to the punch?"

"I'm not a pretty boxer, but I'm strong. I've got loads of videos of myself and have to watch them, but I don't like it. I can see where and how I could be better with timing and movement. Now, I've got to improve those things but I mustn't forget my best quality, my strength in the punch. Of course I practise it, but that side of things really came naturally. It's the other things I've got to work on.

"As for Tyson, I've watched him a lot too. He's never met a boxer like me. He's on a crest of a wave right now, but he's got to come down some time."

We seemed to be drawn back into talking about the proposed September fight with Tyson. I knew that Frank would expect and hope to win, but I thought I'd show my honest doubts (how I'd love to be proved wrong) and ask him what he might do if he lost.

"I might retire, because I'm not going to end up a stepping-stone boxer for others to make their way to the top. I've got to get the money together that I need first though. I've just bought a house in Spain, which is great. I'd love to spend more time with my family really.

"I've got two little girls, Rachel who's six years old, and Nicola who's two. And their Mum, Laura, I don't know how old she is. I've not spent enough time with them in the past.

"I never had much as a child and want to get myself sorted out first so I don't go back to being like I was. I'll have to see what's happening once Terry has had his bit and Mrs Thatch has had hers."

Frank's personality, at least the equal of his enormous boxing ability, is likely to ensure that he can look after himself and his family in the future. There's no doubt that his wishes are genuine. As I walked back to my car through the East End streets I sensed the potential harshness and rawness of life there. For me, this part of the capital only means Dirty Den and a couple of easy points off the Hammers. But I'd react differently if it was home. It's not that you'd want to run from the place, but you'd want to have that option. Not many people do.

For Frank, life is all about the future. He's already a "Great Briton", no doubt, and likely to grow in stature as the years go by. We all look forward to sharing that future with him.

146

Virginia Wade

1977 and all that

Virginia Wade played her first Wimbledon in 1961 at the age of sixteen. She was to spend almost twenty-five years as Britain's top-ranked player. Her first big success was the 1968 US Open, but she had to wait until 1977 – Jubilee year and the Centenary Wimbledon – before she won the coveted ladies' singles title. Virginia was the first woman to be elected to the committee of the All-England Club, in 1982. An MBE award in 1969 was followed by the OBE in 1986. She retired from competition in 1985, after twenty-four consecutive Wimbledons, and now works mostly as a television commentator.

*S*uccessful British tennis players are as rare as Everton victories at Anfield. In fact, only one name comes to mind when looking at the recent history of the game in this country: that of Virginia Wade. She, alone, has held the flag for Britain in a period when we have had a couple of also-rans, several might-have-beens and, to be cruelly honest, a score of no-hopers.

But, if we are to be frank, could not Virginia Wade's career have reached even greater heights than it did? Should she not have been able to clinch more than the one Wimbledon singles title? Well, rather than invent theories about her behind her back, rather than go the way that the press sometimes choose to go, namely finding reasons to knock anyone that is successful, I thought I'd best ask her the question myself. There's no doubt that Virginia Wade has been one of the great British figures in sport. . .but could her achievement have been even greater?

Virginia Wade had kindly agreed to an interview, choosing her favourite Italian restaurant as a venue, because she's happy to oblige. On the chosen day she had many other commitments, not least the launch of her new instructional video, *Virginia Wade's Class*, but she still found time to help an old friend and to talk about sport. She's that kind of person, and sometimes wishes that she had been asked to do a few more things for her sport and her country – but more of that later. For now, let's return to the first question. A bit unkind, perhaps, but she wouldn't expect me to beat about the bush.

"No, I don't mind you asking me," was her helpful response, "because I know that many other people have thought it. . .and I've been asked it before so don't worry. Yes," she continued, "I feel that I could have won Wimbledon four or five times, if only things had been different. I'm not regretful and I don't worry about what might have happened but I suppose my main emotion is frustration. I'm a little bit frustrated that I didn't achieve my full potential, and I am very, very frustrated that others, after me, haven't been able to follow in my footsteps. Having made a breakthrough and achieved the recognition and support for tennis that we did, somehow it's all melted away."

Her frustration is so understandable. If I was talking to Bjorn Borg I would be able to point to all those great Swedish players that have followed in his footsteps. Borg's victories at Wimbledon and around the world sparked his nation into a wholesale enthusiasm for the game. Many more courts were established, scores more coaches were employed and thousands more people took up the game. The result of this is that Sweden is probably the foremost tennis nation in the world, a fact testified to by their recent record in the Davis Cup. The same situation applies to Boris Becker. The young Wimbledon champion was thrust into the limelight by the enthusiastic aggression and lightning reactions of his natural game. And where he led, the rest of his country has not been slow to follow. Tennis is very big in Germany at the moment and the pundits tell us that Steffi Graf is only the first spark from the volcano – the real explosion of new, young hopefuls is yet to come. So, why not Britain? Why am I unable to acclaim Virginia Wade not only as the great player that she was, but also as the leader of a great era in British tennis when our women, and even our men, bore all before them?

Whenever I think about the problem I can feel a sense of frustration too. As a Brit, first and foremost, I would have loved to have seen Virginia Wade follow her 1977 triumph up with four or five more wins. And how nice it would be to welcome Andrew Castle or Jeremy Bates on to *A Question of Sport* as winners of tournaments around the world and ranked in the international top ten – instead of the rather apologetic "leading British player" tag we have to make do with. It's not as if we're trying to produce world-class skiers or baseball players, sports where we don't have the facilities and the tradition. After all, we've played tennis long enough in this country. We used to have champions, male and female. And if Sweden and Germany can do it, why can't we?

Virginia, I'm sure, sensed my growing anger and suggested that we order some lunch. She must have known that eating normally keeps me quiet for a while. I must admit, I felt like dragging my tennis kit out of the back of the car and offering myself up as a British hopeful. But to talk only in terms of failure is wrong. There may have been disappointments and frustrations in Virginia's career, true, but she's also had her share of success. And today, as broadcaster and coach, she's clearly busily and happily involved in her beloved sport of tennis. So while not wishing to leave the subject of British shortcomings altogether, it was time to talk about 1977 and all that.

"I knew I could win that year," she explained, "and when I heard that the Queen was coming to present the trophy I knew that I *had* to win. I could just see myself walking forward to receive the trophy from Her Majesty. I actually think that my ability to visualise my success was part of the reason why I won. There were moments in the competition that year when I felt I wasn't playing very well, but I still had that picture in my mind of me getting my hands on the shield."

"But was that something you had always been looking forward to?" I asked.

"No, not really. I suppose I hadn't really thought much about winning Wimbledon before I started playing professionally. It wasn't as if it was a distant dream, it just didn't really exist for me as an ambition, not at first, at least. I could always see a little way ahead, but never that far."

I was interested in Virginia's answer. For some of us in sport the goals are set early in life, for others the way to success is up a ladder, one step at a time and not really knowing where the top is. From the first day I knew what an England football shirt looked like I knew I wanted to wear one. When I got my first cap it was, quite literally, a dream come true. I had always wanted to play for England – and at last I made it. And I know a lot of people in sport, particularly football, are the same. They want to play for their country, they want to appear in an FA Cup Final, they want to win a League Championship and so on. It doesn't mean they stop when they reach their goal, and it doesn't mean they've failed if they don't actually get there, but the ambition serves as a motivator and a source of energy when times are hard. But clearly this isn't the same for everybody. For Virginia it was definitely one step at a time.

"When I started," Virginia continued, "it was simply a case of banging a ball up against a wall. In fact I was pretty good at all ball games when I was very young. I liked catching and throwing and tried my hand at all sorts of games. It all seemed to come quite naturally. But when I had a tennis racquet put in my hand it suddenly all seemed to make sense. After that it was tennis, tennis and more tennis. I used to drive my parents mad by the constant sound of the ball against the wall. The time the wall was painted white was the worst! Perhaps they thought it was kill or cure, but they gave me ten tennis lessons for my eleventh birthday. After that, there was no looking back."

"And was the path to the top fairly straightforward after that?" I asked.

"Well, not difficult, just a little roundabout. You see, I was living in South Africa at the time and fairly soon ran out of good opponents. The serious playing population there was not enormous and I was sent to England when I was fifteen. The problem then was not one of opponents but of coaches.

"Looking back, I don't think people understood my game well enough. At fifteen I was playing more of a man's game, serve and volley. My opponents were much more conservative and wanted to rally from the line, rarely coming forward. I needed somebody who appreciated my strengths for what they were and who could build on those while, at the same time, could correct the weaknesses in my game. I also needed a coach I could talk to.

"I'm not saying that the coaching was bad for me, but it could have been better. This brings me back to the point I made earlier. With good coaching I believe I could have won Wimbledon before I did, and more times than I did."

I didn't want to ask Virginia about weaknesses, still feeling that now was the time to talk about success, but Virginia was happy and forthright enough to continue the theme.

"Looking at my game, I shouldn't have been allowed to reach the age I did without paying attention to my poor temperament. Just telling me not to lose my temper and not let bad mistakes affect my game was not enough. I needed a method of tackling the problem, a means to encourage a better response to the tense and trying moments of a match.

"One can look at the requirements of the game at the highest level as being good physical ability, a range of skills and a sound psychological approach. Coaches worked on the physical side; that was no problem. I had most of the skills and I was coached in those I lacked. But, as for my temperament, it was never seen as being a problem and therefore went unchecked, spoiling many possible victories for me."

As she spoke I saw those agonising moments again, those matches lost when they should have been won, those tight situations when you just knew that Virginia was the better player but, at the same time, knew she wasn't going to win. Dan Maskell used to groan for us all as the volley slapped into the top of the net or a drive was overhit by a few precious inches. Did Virginia feel the frustration that we all experienced?

"Yes. I knew that I could win those matches, and sometimes, of course, I did. But there were times when I just threw victories away. It was this matter of temperament again."

"Do you feel that you lacked a killer instinct?" I asked.

"No. Not that simple. I don't think I had gained enough from my previous defeats to enable me to take control of the situation. Defeat in sport is an important part of the process. You have to learn how to cope with the disappointment of defeat and you must learn how to profit from it.

"In this country," Virginia was now choosing her words very carefully, "I don't think we are taught how to lose properly. It's something that we should make part of general coaching. We are told how to be good losers, but that's no good. We need to think about gaining something from every situation – defeats as well as victories."

I found this an interesting idea. There is no doubt that defeat was a great motivator for me. And others have said it too. The fear of losing can be all the player needs to give him an edge over his opponents. When you read the football magazines and they ask players what they hate most they normally say either injuries or losing. . .or playing at Luton. Losing is what automatically springs to mind as one of the worst things in football. If I was a manager and a player of mine said he didn't mind losing I would know I had a problem.

Virginia had more than a fear of losing to trouble her. Every time she competed at Wimbledon she had the entire British population playing every shot with her. Did this ever bother her?

"It didn't bother me, but I was conscious of it. It was flattering but I wished, sometimes, that there were others who could take the pressure off a bit. I think it's fair to say that my game improved slightly when Sue Barker came along!"

The mention of Sue Barker's name brought us back to the topic of what came after Virginia. Why did she feel that we didn't develop, as a tennis nation, after her 1977 triumph?

"The first thing is that the Lawn Tennis Association didn't grow with the game. My victory was part of it, but there were other factors too that were helping the game to grow in the later seventies. There were great players around in both the men's and women's game. This led to some titanic clashes that captured the imagination. Players like Borg, McEnroe, Connors and so on were great players and a great draw to the public. The Wimbledon authorities, also, really got their act together and produced huge profits from the championships. But somehow the game at large never capitalised on all this.

"I know that money doesn't go far when you're talking about indoor facilities. However, I don't think it was just a matter of building courts. We needed a better structure for the game in Britain. We needed better coaches staying in this country. Do you know, I can go to almost any country in the world and see British coaches thriving. For many reasons, not just financial, there was never a real encouragement to stay here.

"I can never put my finger on one reason but can only think of instances where I know we could have done better. For example, I won other major tournaments apart from Wimbledon all around the world. But I was never asked to help with the development of our younger players. I could have told them a lot about the business of actually winning. This upset me a little. I think it comes back to the 'structure' as I said before. There didn't seem to be a plan and today we are as far back as ever in world terms."

This I knew to be true. In the course of my work I come across a lot of professional sports men and women. Whoever they are they get my full support. Professional sport is one of the hardest jobs to take on, but it can also be the most rewarding. So I am always happy to meet people from sport, especially if they're young and even more so if they're British and are about to go out and beat the rest of the world. But I have to say the young tennis players of today, especially the women, do not inspire me with a great deal of confidence.

Don't get me wrong on this. I'm not jumping on a bandwagon of criticism. I want them to succeed as much as anyone, probably more than anyone. Somehow, though, they just don't seem to be the right material. Who out of Annabel Croft, Sarah Gomer, Jo Durie and Anne Hobbs is going to win Wimbledon? I'd be the first one over the surrounding wall and onto the Centre Court to cheer, but it isn't going to happen. I suppose this is why Virginia is still the number one representative of British tennis, even in her retirement from playing. Without trying to embarrass her, I put this point to Virginia.

"I came from a time when there were good players around in Britain. Before me, and overlapping with my playing days, were Christine Trueman, Ann Jones and Angela Mortimer. And, of course, there were some fabulous players on the international scene too. It was much more open then, with Margaret Court probably the best I played against, but others like Billie Jean King, Evonne Cawley and Chrissie Evert in her early days all able to turn it on and win tournaments."

"Was Margaret Court your hardest opponent?" I asked.

"Yes. If you look at our record we probably played twelve times and I won about three. I must also mention Maria Bueno. She was a simply gorgeous player to watch and a very hard opponent too. But Margaret was the hardest."

"So," I decided to raise the issue one more time, "why aren't the Crofts, the Hobbses, the Gomers and the Duries of this world going out and winning tournaments?"

"If I had the complete answer I'd be only too happy to tell. I think it's a combination of factors. The coaching isn't as good as it could be, the psychological approach is hardly ever considered. The girls aren't prepared in the right way. This applies to their lifestyle as well as their tennis. Going round the world playing tournaments week in, week out can be very disorientating. The girls tend to lose their sense of roots or belonging. It's a transient life, they get wrapped up in it and perhaps lose sight of their goals. It's a mental adjustment problem and coaching can help, but I don't think we're giving the right kind of coaching.

"The game is different today, too. Perhaps we haven't moved with the times."

"In what ways it is different?" I was interested in this. One of my contentions is that some of our players are not as fit as their overseas counterparts. Perhaps the game has got quicker and our players have not kept pace.

"The main thing in women's tennis today is the ability to rally from the baseline. It was always very important, but used to be combined with a need to play good approach shots which could then be followed up by an attack at the net. I don't think I ever see a deliberate approach shot these days. What this means is that the shots in the heart of the rally can be looser because they are not going to be punished. There's a greater margin for error. I think this applies to the men's game too although both sexes seem to consider that hitting the cover off the ball is the first requirement."

"And what about fitness?"

"Fitness should never be a problem. You can work on that, but you do need good coaching for this too. There's one top player I know who works very hard on the physical side of her game but never seems to get any fitter. That is a matter for coaching; her advisors should spot this."

To my mind tennis has gone down the same path as football with an over-emphasis on the physical side. Looking back to my fitness during my playing days I don't know whether I would be able to last the full ninety minutes of a top match today. The pace is so fast and furious – which I think is to the detriment of the game. But I know that I would train and work until I was fit enough to last, then I'd worry about trying to slow the game down a bit. You've got to be able to compete on equal terms before you can begin to impose your own game.

As Virginia and I came to the end of our lunch we were left reflecting again on what might have been. But we must never lose sight of what has been achieved. Looking at Virginia across the table I could almost hear again those magic words: "That's it, she's done it", words that always send me back to Centre Court, June 1977, and a day when a dream was fulfilled and a nation rose to acclaim one of its most popular champions.

Nigel Mansell

so near yet so far

Britain's most experienced Formula One racing driver, for the last three years he has been one of the top drivers in the world. In 1986 Mansell was denied the world title when a burst tyre in the final Grand Prix of the season at Adelaide cost him the race and very nearly his life. In 1987 he again suffered a blow to his dreams when he crashed in practice for the Japanese Grand Prix. Thirty-three-year-old Mansell started Formula One racing in 1980 with Lotus and achieved his first victory in the European Grand Prix at Brands Hatch in 1985. Outside motor racing, Mansell is a keen golfer and has ambitions of playing in a major golfing tournament.

As soon as I arrived I spotted the man I had come to talk to: Nigel Mansell, standing on the edge of the practice putting green with a golf club tucked under one arm and his young son, Leo, held firmly in the other. His wife, Rosanne, was chatting to their daughter Chloe while Nigel spoke to a couple of fellow golfers. He looked completely relaxed. From what I know of the man, I suspect he was completely happy too.

The beauty of this scene, set on a crisp summer's day in early August, could not have been a greater contrast to the pictures reaching our television sets just a few days before. The British nation had watched with pride and delight as Nigel Mansell had won a spectacular victory over his team-mate, yet rival, Nelson Piquet, to take his third successive British Grand Prix and to put himself in firm contention for the 1987 Drivers' Championship. On that famous day it seemed that most of the 200,000 or so crowd had poured onto the track to surround Mansell's car and to give their hero a welcome he would never forget.

I wondered how deliberate a choice it had been to make golf a main recreation away from the racing circuits. Some fast men choose fast sports for their relaxation, water-skiing, power-boating and the like, but for Nigel the noise and bustle of the pits is replaced by the calm and charm of the clubhouse, the oil-smeared black of the track is substituted by the soft and manicured green of the fairway.

We had agreed to chat over lunch at the beautiful St Pierre Golf Club, just outside Chepstow, where Nigel was helping a BMW car promotion by playing as a guest in a dealer/customer national competition. Was this really work? Was this kind of life something he had looked forward to when he had started out?

"The answer to the first question is definitely 'no'. I love my golf and it's a great opportunity to spend time with my family. The only hard part about it is getting out of the rough, something that seems to be necessary all too often. The answer to the second question must also be 'no'." As he said this he looked around at just what his position at the very top of his sport had provided for him. A magnificent lunch spread awaited, where he was guest of honour; waiting to talk to him were top executives from BMW and his own personal assistant; waiters, waitresses and guests whispered to one another and craned their necks to get a better view of the hero in their midst; and a middle-aged man dressed in golfing attire quietly and modestly hovered in the wings, hoping for a chance to ask for an autograph. "I just never thought about the trappings. All I wanted to do was win." As he said this he extricated himself from the group and took up the pen and paper from the middle-aged man, signing an autograph with a smile and a flourish before taking his place at the table. Exit one very happy and grateful fan.

Whether Nigel had thought about the fruits of victory or not there was no mistaking the fact that this was a far cry from his beginnings in motor sport. His wasn't exactly a rags-to-riches story but more of a riches-to-rags-to-riches epic. He started when he was seven and was racing go-karts competently and competitively by the ripe old age of nine. At eleven he was in the British team but, although racing was important, it had to be a pastime and not a way of life.

At twenty Nigel was working for British Aerospace and on the verge of a managerial career within the company. Unfortunately for the future British number one, and probably for British Aerospace, motor sport was becoming a way of life and work was becoming the pastime. It was crunch time, and a gentle guiding hand from his employers (they actually suggested that his heart was in racing and not in management) led to a full-time commitment to racing – and winning. At this stage the rags figure quite heavily in the story, as Rosanne will be only too happy to tell you. Three weeks into his new career Nigel suffered a broken neck. Not too long after this setback, and already back in the driver's seat, the house was sold for £12,000. This went on four races; the money was gone in just five weeks and Nigel felt he was no further forward. Could things get worse? Just a bit. From their own home the Mansells moved into rented accommodation and then sharing with family. This was a recipe for disaster as many unfortunate marriages will bear witness. For Nigel and Rosanne it was the hardest time, arguments and recriminations, disillusion and despondency. So what kept them going?

"I just knew that we would make it," Nigel explained as our lunch started. "It can only be described as a gut feeling. I'm not talking about winning world championships or being rated as British and world number one. All I thought about was just winning races, each and every race. After we had won one my mind would turn to the next. If we kept on winning, eventually people would start taking notice." And, of course, they did. The hard days were eventually left behind. The money, most welcome, and the fame, much appreciated, started to accumulate.

However, it wasn't until the famous Grand Prix victory at Brands Hatch in 1986 that Britain and the world finally and fully recognised Mansell for the champion he really is. The pressure that day must have been enormous, with the largest Grand Prix crowd ever assembled in Britain all watching one man and expecting, not just hoping for but *expecting*, victory. Victory was duly served up, but at what a cost to nerves and stamina. Today, as he did with the assembled guests at St Pierre on that August day, Nigel is pleased, but not cocky, when he announces he is one of the best four or five drivers in the world. "I always knew I could be very good but it did take a long time for others to see it in me. Winning a

Grand Prix, and then winning my second British Grand Prix, really killed off any doubts, although, of course, you still get a few critics who reckon I've been lucky or that I'm not really that good. For those people I like to let my record speak for itself. We have won more Grands Prix than James Hunt, three British Grand Prix victories and, to date, pole position in six of the eight Grands Prix this year."

That kind of record may silence most of the critics but it doesn't deter the bright sparks who just fancy a race. "I get plenty of them, young lads who just reckon that I'm not all I'm cracked up to be. But you put me, back-to-back, with anyone at all – and you could stake as much as you wanted on me and your money would be safe." Now this didn't sound like the modest Nigel I had been speaking to for the last half an hour. But then again, this was neither talk about the past nor talk about golf; this was now and this was business. The rest of the table sensed the urgency and competitiveness in Nigel's voice; their own conversations quietened as they strained to listen. What they heard next actually brought a complete and stunned silence to the table.

"And the reason I can say that with confidence," said Nigel, referring to his boast, "is because I've been in the business so long. I have come up the long way and the hard way. I have got the necessary experience; I'm better at racing, better with cars and better at cheating." It was this word "cheating" that caused the silence. The other lunch guests laid down their forks, put down their glasses and gave up the pretence of having their own separate conversations. Had they heard correctly?

Nigel had sensed the interest and had comfortably predicted my next question. "When I say 'cheating'" (he began his answer before I spoke), "I mean pushing the rules and regulations to the limit. Actually everybody does that, what we do is try to push them just beyond the limit and see how far we can go before we get reined in." The table relaxed, meals and conversations were resumed. Nigel, as we all knew, didn't cheat. He just indulged in that British pastime of a little bit of gamesmanship. I was able to relate to that. I told Nigel of the tricks of the trade that the great Shanks would indulge in. He would never have supported cheating – at least not if anybody was looking. I recalled that before matches he would make sure he found out a little about the referee. He passed on the information to me so I could have a friendly chat with the man as we shook hands before kick-off. I would ask how his wife was, if his dog was better, how his roses were coming along. It not only made the other skipper feel a bit inferior but it's hard to book a guy who's just asked after your sick mother!

Talking about football referees led, almost instinctively, to talk about the administrators in motor racing. Like many of the officials in soccer the men in FISA and in other organising bodies are well-meaning amateurs. They have to be treated with the utmost care. How did Nigel get along with them? Did they not get in the way of his driving ambition and his overriding professionalism?

"I have simply learned to live with them. I've been fined for shunts that weren't my fault and I've been reprimanded for insignificant incidents. But once you let these things worry you then you're wasting precious energy. I've no time for people who are not positive. I'll give advice and help to anyone who really wants to succeed but I will not spend hours listening to grumblers or getting involved in squabbles or discontent that has no bearing on my winning motor races. Since I've been at the top I've not been bothered by officialdom and I hope I don't really bother them."

Nigel's live-and-let-live approach to officials does not extend to the press. "I love 'em," he announced with irony so strong I reckon they must have felt the sting in Fleet Street. "When I was first in racing some of them actually asked for backhanders to say nice things about me. My rule at the time was to leave it to them; they could write what they liked about me, good or bad, but I wasn't going to pay for it. I probably could have benefited from some more press attention in my early days, but that's no way to get it.

"I simply stuck with the journalists from the quality papers and let the rest get what they could. Unfortunately, even a fair and unbiased attitude doesn't mean you are free from unfounded rumour and unfair criticism. Most recently Chris Hill, a journalist, has written a book about me. During the course of it he didn't speak to me once; the result is a load of inaccuracies and, quite frankly, nonsense. There's one really funny error about Rosanne – but I don't think I want you to note it now. We'll let him find out for himself!

"I don't want to break my own rules and start getting negative about it all. The press have a job to do; they could probably do it a bit better, that's all."

Nigel had again referred to attitude, the importance of being positive, the damaging effect of a negative outlook. I wondered whether this was the key to Nigel's success. Did he feel it was the magic ingredient that set him apart from others?

"Actually, no." The reply was very straightforward. "I have had the opportunity to look back at my career and, in particular, to look at those people who fell by the wayside as we went along the route to the top. I reckon the key has been taking the next step, always being prepared to go a little bit further. Some friends, who at the time could give me a very close race, were not prepared to sell their houses, spend the time away from their families, give up their social lives or make any of the other

161

necessary sacrifices. I don't blame them but they mustn't complain about not reaching the top. Assuming you've got the natural ability you must be prepared to push yourself to the limit – and then go a bit further. That's my formula."

Our lunch nearly finished, some guests came round for autographs. This gave me an opportunity to think about Mansell's recipe for success. It certainly struck a chord with me. I remember, once I had decided that I wanted to make a career out of soccer, that I would let nothing stand in my way. On the Friday evening of a match weekend I would leave Barbara and the children to book myself into a hotel just to ensure I got my sleep. This was particularly necessary when the children were young and likely to wake in the night. I even took a few sleeping pills in those days, just to get the hours I reckoned I needed. And that is quite a confession from a man who's only taken two aspirin tablets in his whole life! You just have to go for it. If you want to reach the top – and stay there – then you must be prepared to make the effort, no matter what the cost.

Were there other similarities I could relate to? Yes, there was the love of family life and the love of golf. I am happy to confirm that both Nigel and I derive immeasurable pleasure and satisfaction from our families, but I'm less happy to make a comparison of our golfing achievements. Nigel's handicap has recently come down from four to two despite the lack of encouragement from Frank Williams, Mansell's team boss, who reckons golf should be taken up when you're about ninety. At my present rate of improvement I'll be about ninety before I reach any standard at all.

Like me Nigel also seemed to be a happy man. I watched him smiling and laughing as he chatted to his golfing partners and those seeking autographs. When he returned to our conversation I asked him about this. Was he only able to relax and enjoy a joke when away from work, or were there laughs on the Grand Prix circuit? "Work is much more intense and that often leads to a different sort of humour. Yes, there's great fun to be had in the business, but it is a business and that places constraints on everybody. Mind you, it didn't stop me enjoying a good joke at the expense of a driver (who we won't mention by name!) a couple of years back in Spain. I was right behind him for two, maybe three, laps. Right on his tail, bobbing and weaving, trying to sell him a dummy so I could pass. He was racing well but couldn't really concentrate on his own driving because he was so conscious of the car right up his backside. We came to one sharp right-hand corner and I really put the pressure on. I have never laughed so much – the driver was watching me so intently, trying to predict which way I was going to go, that he completely forgot to take the corner and went straight off the track.

"I can remember too when, at the Paul Ricard track in France early in the 1987 season, we were leading from the start, and after a lap I knew that, barring the odd burst tyre or loose bolt, I could win. I thought I would sharpen them up in the pits a little so announced to all those listening on the car-to-pits link: 'It's OK. We're going to win. You can all piss off home now!' What I didn't know was that the sponsors were listening in too!"

Nigel could clearly make a living for himself out of after-dinner speaking. He seemed completely at home in these surroundings. Perhaps it could become all too alluring and sap his ambition? Yet again Nigel appeared to read my mind, and before my question was complete the answer was there: "The ambition is still as strong as ever, to win races and to be at the top. I'm not talking about the championship now. If that comes it will be nice but I don't need it. I know I'm as good as anyone and better than almost everyone." And as Nigel said it, we all believed it. The truth of the statement shone through him. He *really* didn't mind about not winning the Drivers' Championship because he *really* did know he was the best. But, of course, I couldn't leave the subject without touching on the now famous incident of the burst tyre in Adelaide which cost him the 1986 championship. All he needed to do at the time of the incident was complete the race – the blow-out, apart from threatening his life, had the effect of ruining a whole season's work. "I look on it now as an education. It was a disappointment, in fact it was a bloody shame, but what could I do? I knew I had done enough and one bit of bad luck cost me. It's no good getting all screwed up about that. We just had to start again."

That last sentence summed up the man in many ways, not least because of the way he used the word "We" instead of "I". I've listened to enough so-called stars to get sick to death of "I did this", "I did that" and, most commonly, "I'm going to do such-and-such". It's so refreshing to hear somebody actually ascribe his success to others in the very way he speaks. "We", in Nigel's language, has many meanings. It can refer to his family, his racing team, his sponsors and, at St Pierre that day, his golf team. It's an important part of his make-up, and a very likeable part of it too.

The idea of being part of a team is important to Nigel in keeping his ambition sharp. Perhaps if it had only been him he would have tried less hard in a few really tight races. But that's not even a remote possibility when you're representing your racing team and your sponsors. You let yourself down and you let them down. The Canon–Williams–Honda team is very important to Nigel. "I definitely do feel loyal and, naturally, I know the members of the team very well. We've done the hard work and now should be fine-tuning for victory. I wouldn't want to start all over again, forming new relationships and getting used to a new set-up. When

I'm racing out there I'm racing for the whole team. That's what stops the ambition from being blunted at the moment."

Our conversation was drawing to a close, the golfers were getting ready to move off. It struck me that no one had mentioned the one topic we all think about when discussing motor racing – the possibility of a serious accident. But how can you talk to a man about his chances of dying as he sits there, in the prime of his life, surrounded by his family and friends? Clearly, you cannot. You must not. And that must be the way that Nigel Mansell, and all the others involved in his 200 mph way of life (and death) deal with the problem. You never think about it. You know fear and you are careful but you don't know death so you don't give it a second thought.

So my last questions were on ambition. What's left? "Simple, I want to qualify for the British Open Golf Championship!" Nigel's reply was deadly serious and who would dare bet against him achieving that ambition. Rosanne just hopes that it won't involve selling the house. "Actually my friend Greg Norman has arranged for me to have a wild-card entry into the Australian Open this year. Unfortunately the date for the tournament is the same as for the arrival of our next child. It's something of a problem." I looked at Rosanne and decided that silence was the best policy. By the time this book is published we'll know how the vote went – my suspicion is that Nigel is hoping for the child to arrive a few days early! He deserves a bit of luck.

John Lowe

the first among equals

John Lowe from Derbyshire has been a professional darts player since 1976. Since then he has amassed over 1000 trophies, although he did not start playing darts until he was twenty-one. One of the most consistent players on the circuit, the 1987 World Darts Champion is also a former World Masters Champion and an England international.

I think it's inevitable that, before you go somewhere for the first time or meet somebody new, you form some kind of picture in your mind. When Liverpool were playing in Europe we would often come up against players or teams we had heard about but never seen. My imagination would run riot; I could conjure up fiery and swarthy Latins – who then turned out to be cool and blond Scandinavians, or iron-jawed and unsmiling East Germans who, on the night, were real softies (this didn't happen often!).

Perhaps I should have learned from my experiences, but no, on going to meet John Lowe at his home my mind was full of mental pictures. I saw his lounge stuffed full of memories from around the world; there would be mounted sets of darts, cups, shields and piles of videos of John's great victories arranged neatly around the television. On the walls there would be scores of photographs of John, either with other great players or with the stars of sport and entertainment who like nothing better than a game of darts. And, of course, there would be dart boards. One or two would be hanging in the office, one mounted in the lounge – and I think I even expected to find the front door with glass in the shape of a board.

How wrong can you be? Not since I bought Privy Star, my first race horse, has my judgement been so awry. There was not a dart board, trophy, picture or even a dart in sight. So I decided to ask John about it – surely there was something to remind him of his sport when he was at home?

"I've got a games room," he answered in his warm Derbyshire accent, "with fifteen hundred trophies in it. I sometimes go and look at them. But it's my work, see, and I don't want to bring it home with me."

"And what about a dart board? You must need one for practising."

"Well yes, I've got one in the games room but it's mostly my children who use it. I'll only play on it if I'm practising for a major tournament and I haven't been out doing exhibitions. I don't really need to practise now, just warm up."

No practice? This sounds like a good game for some footballers I could think of. I think John noticed my smile because he went back to the point about practising.

"If I'm really busy I can play in about two hundred exhibitions in a year in addition to the major tournaments. So I'm getting in the hours on the ockey. I know how and where to throw so it's not a business of learning new tricks. No, I just need to warm up, get in the groove."

"And you're really happy to leave it all behind?"

"It's no problem. I have to relax, and home is where I do it. You probably know yourself, Emlyn, what it's like. You can put it out of your mind for so long but, eventually, it begins to take over. I'm all right sat

168

home. I'm not thinking about the next match; instead, I'm out in the garden, chatting to family, watching television, that kind of thing. Then, once I'm on my way to the tournament, the nerves begin to build. The bigger the tournament and the larger the crowd, the more I like it. I need to get fired up to produce my best."

I did know what he meant. And I think most sports stars are the same. I've always needed my home and, quite separately, the stage on which to perform. Although I would always play in smaller games if given the opportunity, it was the big match that brought the best out in me. It's been explained to me as the ability to use the extra nervous energy or adrenalin to the maximum effect. Some people would get knotted up with all the emotional turmoil that a cup final, local derby or, in John's case, major championship, could bring. The top players, however, can channel their extra energy into whatever they want, whether it be that extra dose of concentration or the necessary speed for the last lap. At the end of the day, though, everybody needs somewhere they can relax. For John and me, it's home that counts. Other performers, as we can read every Sunday, find the disco or the night club the place to get away from it all.

None of these thoughts about major championships and coping with nerves seemed to be going through John's mind as we spoke. I have rarely come across a man looking so relaxed and self-assured. Admittedly he wasn't playing that night, but John exuded confidence – I certainly didn't see him suffering from the dreaded "dartitis" that had affected some of his closest rivals.

But what is all this talk of major championships, nerves and "dartitis"? Isn't darts just a game you play, for a bit of fun, in your local pub or club? Isn't it an amateur game, a million miles away from the hustle and bustle of the megabuck sports like soccer, golf and tennis? The answer is – it used to be. Until John Lowe came on the scene. In many ways the history of modern professional darts is the history of John Lowe. John is not only the father of the modern game, he's its favourite son as well. So, how did it all begin? I asked John this question and soon had another of my preconceptions shattered.

"It was luck, or perhaps fate should I say. I was out with my girlfriend Diane, who's now my wife, down at the Butcher's Arms not a hundred yards from here. We were watching some mates play a friendly game. One of them had to go to the toilet and, as he left the bar, passed me his darts. 'Take my go for me John,' he said. I did and found it quite easy. I took his next turn too. And then played a whole game. The next evening I came back and played some more. And the next evening. . .and so on. It grew from there, from a simple request to take somebody's turn to the position where I must throw millions of darts every year.

"That first game was twenty-one years ago; I was twenty-one at the time. I was in a good job. Apart from spending time with Diane most of my time was taken up with motor bikes; I was a complete bike freak. Darts was the last thing on my mind. I know that I would never have started without that bit of luck."

I wondered what would have happened if John's friend had returned from the toilet in time to take his own throw? I expect Eric Bristow sometimes wonders that too.

"And did it simply grow from that first game?" I asked John.

"Yes, although I never expected it to take off in quite the way it did. I played matches and tournaments and kept winning, but it wasn't until the arrival of television that the prize money started growing, the popularity increased and the top players started to become known in every home. Before television I was well known locally, but not nationally. It was Freddie Trueman's lunch-time television programme about pub games, called *Indoor League* I think, that was the turning point.

"In that show we played all sorts of games: bar billiards, pool, dominoes, cribbage, etc. However, it was darts that was the most popular and it soon was being televised in its own right. Of course, it was just right for television. Darts is a simple game to score and the rules are easy to follow. The action is pretty fast and there are always tight finishes for the armchair fan to get excited about. To my mind, however, the best thing about the television boom was the fact that the top players at the time were such varied people.

"Let's be honest. I have a style of play that appeals to some people and rubs others up the wrong way. What's certain is that the television audience wouldn't get a lot of fun out of watching a dozen John Lowes in every tournament. They want variety, and got it with the players who first featured in television darts. People like Alun Evans, Tony Brown, Cliff Lazarenko and, soon after, Eric Bristow, made compulsive watching."

John had a good point. You don't get characters in your soap operas as good as those he mentioned. Jocky Wilson's got more about him than the entire cast of some soaps.

When I've talked to most of the other stars in this book I've found out who were the major influences on their careers: to whom they looked up, who inspired them. In John's case this was not a relevant question. There was nobody quite like John in the pre-television era. I had checked the record books and seen that big darts tournaments had existed before John. The games were largely between amateurs and mostly confined to the South of England. The *News of the World* hosted the British Championship, and it attracted a crowd of 17,000 in 1939 to see Marmaduke Breckon beat Jim Pike. Each player represented a pub with

170

side betting being the major financial interest. Through this kind of tournament the rules for darts started to become standardised nationwide and this allowed more competition between the regions. But this had little relevance for John. He was self-taught, self-improved and quickly became the model for other players rather than somebody else's pupil.

With the possible exception of Jim Pike, John and his contemporaries were the first major names in the sport. Many of those "pioneers" are still playing and this makes darts different in one respect from most other sports: at the present time it's still not possible to argue who was the greatest of them all. The major players are still putting their reputations on the line in tournaments throughout the world. Until one or more of them finally retire there can be no completed records of achievement. John, for example, has appeared in eight World individual finals (actually only winning twice) and this obviously puts him into contention for the all-time best tag. But who's to say that John hasn't got another half-dozen final appearances left in him? What would that do to the record books?

It would be unfair to talk about John Lowe in terms of record books alone. He's not that kind of player. He's been the figurehead of darts for such a long time, a complete ambassador for the sport and for Britain. His reputation is one of good manners, good sportsmanship and, perhaps less flatteringly, one of a dour competitor. I wanted to ask John about his approach to the game, but didn't want to suggest he was unexciting. His nickname, both in the game and for the wider public, is "Stoneface". I wondered if he liked that. I could recall at Anfield being known as "Crazy Horse". That I took as a compliment, both because it suited my character and because I was flattered that people should take the trouble to think up a name for me. I'm not sure, though, whether I should have liked to have been called "Stoneface". What about John?

"It's because I don't blink or move my head," he answered simply. "Is it flattering? I don't know, but it's a compliment in the sense that you've got to keep your head still to throw decent darts. And with a stone face, I'm obviously doing something right.

"I'll tell you though," he continued, "I read a golf magazine in which Peter Alliss said that golfers could learn a lot from watching John Lowe. Alliss was talking about keeping one's head still during the swing; that's complimentary but it hasn't helped my golf at all!"

"And do you see yourself as the ambassador of the game?" I asked.

"Not really. I'm a player first and foremost. What I will do, though, is tell the authorities if I think they've got something wrong. The governing body is relatively young and so has a lot to learn. I'm happy to help them."

Perhaps I could sense here that John Lowe was something of a rebel, an anti-authority man. I put this to John straight.

"No, not really," came the straight reply. And I believe him. "Recently the authorities have tried to clean up our act a bit, by simple things like putting the drinks table out of sight of the cameras and banning players from smoking in televised tournaments. I'm happy to support them in that kind of move. I'm also keen to persuade them to spread the money around a bit. At the moment a tournament winner can get, say, £6000 and the next man get only £3000. First-round losers might get just a couple of hundred. I think the differences between top and bottom could be a lot less; this would help out newer players a bit. Sponsors, of course, like to be seen presenting big cheques so change might be slow coming.

"Funnily enough, television rarely shows the presentation of a trophy or a cheque. I might lose my 'Stoneface' image if they showed my smile when I'm picking up a cheque for a few thousand quid.

"Overall, darts is very sporting and I've got little to complain about. You would soon be out on a limb if you started throwing your weight around."

This provided the opening for me to ask about Bristow. Eric Bristow, the "Crafty Cockney", has been the man the press have heralded as the major challenger to John's crown. Some fans would suggest that, in fact, John is the challenger to Eric's crown. Whatever the truth of that, there can be no mistaking the apparent intensity of the rivalry between these two contrasting competitors: Eric, the rather brash extrovert, and John, the calm and collected automaton.

"Most of all it's been a good story," John began. "For almost two years I couldn't beat Eric and the press just loved the atmosphere of a showdown every time we met in a major championship. Then the tables were turned, and poor Eric suffered with dartitis, his inability to actually let go of the dart. Quite frankly he's not a problem at the moment; I know I can take him any time."

"Is there anything personal in it?" I wanted to find out the truth because I know that John could rub me up the wrong way with his approach to victory! If Emlyn Hughes has got to lose, which I never like to accept, then I want the other guy to do the decent thing and shut up about it! John is the great after-match analyst. I've heard him explain exactly when and why his opponent has let him in. If I had been forced to listen to that I think I would have hit him; at least let me suffer my defeat alone. Did this annoy Eric?

"I don't know. The problem is always finding something to say when the cameras are on you. Some players will be led into saying all kinds of things they later regret. I'd rather stick to the game. Take Jocky Wilson, for example. He's told the press how much he drinks and now he's got to live with that every time he opens a paper. But, back to your question, Eric and I compete happily together, and that's about it."

No scandal there. Perhaps I should ask about Jocky.

"My best memory of Jocky," John replied, "was when I had to play him in a deciding leg in an England versus Scotland match in Edinburgh. There were four and a half thousand Jocky Wilsons screaming for an Englishman's blood when it came to the decider. We had to nominate one from me, Dave Whitcombe, Keith Dellar and Eric. I was skipper and the boys nominated me for the one leg, 501, nearest bull to start. I got the bull and stayed ahead of him all the way ending up with 61 to finish. I threw for 25 to leave 36 but scored a bull, leaving 11. Not my best finish! But I threw 3, double 4 to bring complete silence to a hall where, moments before, there had been screaming and cheering. Poor Jocky."

Poor Jocky indeed. Pure magic I thought. I can still remember the times, more than the Scots will care to count, when an English team I've been in has brought a hush to a packed Hampden Park.

As I listened to John talk about his Scottish triumph I sensed an excitement in his voice that had not been there before. Was it winning that drove him on?

"No, it's the losing." His reply was forthright. . .and exactly the same as mine would have been if asked the same question. I didn't need to ask more; I knew what he meant. When we lost with Liverpool I would sometimes sit for over an hour in the dressing room, going over every point of the game, analysing everything that could have been done differently. Then I would get to the car where Barbara would be waiting. She would know not to say anything – just to let me get it out of my system. The only words I would say would be to ask for the sandwich that I knew she would have made for me. Eventually it would pass, but not before I had determined that I would get rid of the feeling the only way possible, by winning the next match, and the next match, and the next. . .

As John and I talked I discovered more and more about why he is so admired in the game. He's got the whole thing in perspective. He knows that he owes all he has to darts – his beautiful home, financial security and the opportunity to travel around the world. But he also knows that it's not the only thing in life. He's absolutely determined to work hard at his game and to put everything he's got into it. But he's equally sure that he's going to retire in five years' time no matter what. I've never seen a man more sure about his retirement, and more determined to quit at the very top.

Being at the top means something in darts. There are seven million competitive players in the United Kingdom and twenty-five million playing worldwide. To be top of that little pile must be quite a feeling. "A bit special," was how John described it. More than just the accolade of being number one, there's also the need to stay in the top sixteen. This means exemption from qualifying tournaments, an important financial consideration.

"Of course," admitted John when we started talking about the future and the threats to John's position as the best-known darts player worldwide, "there are any number of good players coming along. Bob Anderson is the major newcomer, but others like Keith Dellar have forced themselves to the top and have managed to stay there. As I said earlier, I'm giving it five more years and then that's it. But I want to quit at the top and, if this year is anything to go by, I'll just about achieve that final ambition."

"Only five more years? Surely that's too young to retire." I hope Eric Bristow never learns that I tried to dissuade John Lowe from quitting.

"In one sense I see what you mean. But don't forget that there's no closed season in darts. Playing for eleven seasons means playing continuously for eleven years. Apart from the occasional week's holiday, I've not stopped since I started!"

"And what will you miss most?"

"The people. Darts is fun, and most of the people in it work hard at having a good time. And also, I should say, the trips abroad. I've played in some strange places, on North Sea oil rigs, on Thursday Island (Jocky thought it was called 'Thirsty Island') and in Japan. It's not that Japan is funny, but the way they play their darts is a bit strange. We all had to wear suits, were fined if we were late for press conferences and played in front of literally thousands of fans at every venue. It was an amazing experience; I'm sure the future of the game will be heavily influenced by what happens in the Far East."

I realised that I could listen to John talking about his darts all day and all night. Unfortunately we both had other commitments so I contented myself with one last question.

"Apart from ending 'at the top', do you have any specific ambitions remaining?" I asked.

"The nine-dart out on television – again! I remember the fuss when my counterpart, 'The Grinder' Cliff Thorburn, did a televised maximum break 147 in snooker's World Championship. I did the 501 but it wasn't in a major tournament. It's hardly been shown on television at all. I just hope to do it again soon, and make this one the winning leg of the World Championship against Eric Bristow. Seriously, just to do it in a televised, major tournament, that would be something else. I think the key is relax and then, perhaps, rush at it. . .not think too hard about any of the darts. I remember playing with the great Tony Brown once when we decided to play as quickly as we could with a side bet on 180s. I've never thrown them so consistently. In the final I threw eight to his five although I actually lost the match. But now it's the nine-dart finish I'm after at the present."

And who would be surprised if he gets it? Nobody; most players will simply be grateful that it's not scored against them.

As I rose to go I was reminded of my earlier expectations about John's house, and how they were proved to be wide of the mark. But, as I left via the kitchen, I spied the tell-tale sign of the great, yet down-to-earth, champion. On the ironing board, receiving his wife's loving attention, was the famous blue shirt with the name "John Lowe" modestly scrolled across the back. I knew he couldn't leave his work totally behind.

Bill Shankly

a legend among the greats

Bill Shankly rose from humble beginnings to fame as manager of one of the best football clubs in the world. In 1959 he took over from Phil Taylor and began what was to be a glorious era as Liverpool won the League, FA Cup and League again in successive seasons. It was shortly after a second FA Cup triumph that Shankly announced his retirement. Bill Shankly died in 1982 following a heart attack, and his name is commemorated in the Shankly Gates at Anfield. A man of outstanding vision, he transformed Liverpool and offered hope to a city with growing problems. He was awarded an OBE for his services to sport.

*T*his is the chapter I just had to write. Bill, sadly no longer with us, is one of my all-time great "Great Britons". On a personal level he was the guiding hand behind my career. Without him I would never have been captain of England. I owe him an enormous debt. But that's not the sole reason for his inclusion. Bill was larger than that; he was a Great Briton in every sense of the word. He gave so much to the game he loved. He was a great manager of people, he had a wonderful football brain and he was one of the most likeable fellows you could wish to meet. . .providing you didn't say anything against his beloved Liverpool.

I know I couldn't believe it the day that Bill Shankly left Liverpool Football Club, long before he seemed ready to retire, and I can still scarcely believe that "The Boss" is sadly gone. But his memory lives on, of course, both in the club he built and in the hundreds of funny stories and anecdotes attributed to him. He was larger than life and, I like to think, larger than death.

I think Shanks would have been amused had I asked him to be one of the stars interviewed for this book. He probably wouldn't have considered that writing was a proper job, although he was always very good with the press. He also wouldn't have considered himself worthy of inclusion in such exalted company. "Just doing my job," was the way he summed up the magic of his management. His modesty aside though, the interview would have been granted only if it didn't interfere with his work, or mine, for Liverpool. Anything that didn't directly relate to the Club would always come second.

So should I suppose that the interview would have been granted and make it up from there? No. How can I be sure what the man might have said? I wouldn't want to try to put words into his mouth about such personal issues as his greatest moment or biggest disappointment. I don't think anyone, apart from his wife, knew the personal side of Bill that well. It's as a manager of a football club that I knew Bill the longest, and it's in this role of manager that I feel I want to remember him. The question I put to Shanks and the question that I will do my best to answer on his behalf, is how would he have managed my "Great Britons"?

Look at them. I wouldn't have liked to have coped with that lot. Try putting such different personalities as George Best and Nigel Mansell in the same side, and try coping with the attitudes to sport of international performers like David Bryant and Sean Kerly. And how to get the best from Virginia Wade and John Francome? And how to deal with the press when you've got Her Royal Highness The Princess Royal in your team? All these problems, and many more, are the sorts of things I would have wanted to hear about from Bill. And knowing him as well as I did, I think I can hazard a pretty fair guess as to some of his answers and approaches.

Bill was a great team manager, getting the very best from each individual in order to make up his larger-scale plan. He made good players great, and even mediocre players could produce some phenomenal performances under the guiding hand and eye of The Boss. I think that Brian Clough is the only manager on the current scene who's able to match him in this respect. So let's start from the top (in this book that means you can choose any players from the list) and imagine the scene when David Bryant comes into Shanks's office to announce he's hurt himself while gardening and can't play on Saturday. I can just picture the scene now:

"Boss," David would say, timorously.

"Yes," would come the reply in Bill's broad Scottish accent.

"I can't play on Saturday because I slipped whilst wearing my carpet slippers in the garden. I think I've pulled a hamstring as a result of this."

That would have been the end of the conversation unless Bill checked to see if it was April Fool's Day. Bill would have been so completely stunned, just incredulous, that a professional sportsman could take such risks. It would seem inconceivable to him that a player could do anything to jeopardise his place in the team or the chance of a couple of points at the weekend.

I'm pretty sure that the shock would have been so great that the culprit, in our case David Bryant, would have got away without a severe dressing-down. A shaking of the head and a couple of gasps of amazement would have been all that Bill could have managed at the time.

Bill had a garden, but that was Nessie's job. Anything that didn't relate to football was Nessie's job. Relaxation didn't mean digging in the garden. It didn't even mean walking round it and sniffing the roses. Relaxation, to Bill, was only one thing. That was sitting with your feet up while watching television and having a cup of tea. Feet up, above your waist, so the strength drained back into your body.

Bill's code of conduct was fairly straightforward. Relaxation was pretty near the top, and restraint from "troughing" and "pouching", eating and drinking to excess, were also high priorities. It was a simple code and Bill couldn't see any reason why others didn't follow it. Players were being paid, and paid well, to be professional footballers. Therefore they didn't do things that interfered with their paid employment. Simple, and David Bryant would be hiring a gardener, or a wife, next week.

So how would Bill have treated someone like Sean Kerly, a man who didn't have to sacrifice everything because of his amateur status? I'm convinced that Bill would have had a lot of time for Sean. And I know that he would have understood entirely the priorities that exist for Sean. The key to football, and the key to life, for Bill, was to put one hundred per cent into whatever you're doing. It would have worried Bill if Sean didn't put everything into his job as jewellery merchandising manager. All Bill could want from Sean would be total dedication *on* the field of play. Of course, from Sean, he would have got it. Sean and Bill would have gone well together.

Another person whom Bill would have got on well with, but who would have posed different problems, is Virginia Wade. Nobody could miss Ginny's talent, but who could persuade her to realise her full potential? As she so aptly described when she spoke to me, she needed somebody to get hold of her in her formative years. She needed someone to do for her what Shanks did for me.

Ginny's temperament was not quite what it should have been, and that contributed to a number of squandered matches and tournaments. Shanks would have soon appreciated the problem and given her the boost in confidence that seemed to be so badly lacking at times. I can recall a time, shortly after I joined Liverpool, when things didn't seem to be going too well for me. I was a bit quiet, a bad sign for me, and generally feeling a bit down. The Boss spotted me moping about and asked me into the office.

"What's the problem son?" he asked. There was no point in trying to hide things from Shanks, but I gave it a go anyway.

"Nothing, Boss."

"Don't lie son. I can see there's something wrong. Why don't you tell me?"

I knew what was wrong, but it was hard to put it into words. The fact was that Liverpool, when I joined them, had a great squad. They had four players just back from winning the World Cup. They had strong internationals in almost every position and, above all, they were all confident in their ability. I was beginning to worry about mine. What was worse was that I didn't think I had been made to feel that welcome. Of course I could understand it, a highly priced teenager clearly keen to take somebody's place in the team. But I was unhappy about the situation and, try as I might, didn't seem to be able to put things right.

Eventually I found the words to tell Shanks why I was unhappy and what my worries were. He instantly spotted that it was my own confidence that was beginning to take a battering. I would be able to fit in with the other players once I had the confidence to realise I was as good as them. He put it to me like this, a statement from a manager that took real guts and a real appreciation of the problem.

"Son," said Shanks, "don't you worry. If there's any problem with the other players I'll sack the lot of them. You are the future of Liverpool and it's your interests I've got to put first."

That was quite a sensational thing to say. It rocked me, but gave me just the boost I needed. Of course, there were no wholesale sackings; they were never needed. I just grew into a place in the team and let the players' acceptance of me come along when they were ready. It ceased to be a problem.

I like to think that Ginny Wade would have received the same kind of treatment from Shanks. She wouldn't ever have worried about her opponents again because she would have been told that she was the best in the world. Let the opponents do the worrying, would have been Shanks's advice. They'll just roll over for you when you're ready.

During her career, Ginny saw her recurring inability to deal with inferior opponents as a problem. John Francome saw his missed victories and unnecessary falls as something to laugh about. Could Shanks have coped with this approach? That's a difficult one, but I think I know the answer.

Yes, John would have driven Shanks up the wall with his attitude, but one thing would have saved him, his sense of humour. I can picture the scene as John faces up to The Boss following some minor disaster in the saddle. As the rest of my "Great Britons" cower quietly in the corners of the mythical dressing room, John would completely disarm Shanks with some comment about the weather or tomorrow's racing. And even if Bill thought that John was being a bit too disrespectful he'd not be able to resist either the accent or the smile. Basically he would have enjoyed having John around.

If John Francome is the practised master of the warm smile and the beguiling comment, then George Best is the acknowledged inventor of the art form. There's probably not a man I know, and there's certainly not a woman, who could resist him. Even if Shanks occasionally got fed up with excuses and apologies he would have made allowances because of the wee Irishman's genius. There's no doubt in my mind that Shanks would have loved to have Besty in his team. I think the partnership could have worked because George would have been good for Liverpool and Shanks would have been good for George.

This is not to say that Shanks would have tamed Besty; he wouldn't even have tried. But I think George could have fitted into a team plan, something that Liverpool worked to, better than some might imagine. George, after all, was a great fighter on the field. He wanted the ball, and he wanted it back if he lost it. That would have gone down very well at Anfield.

I look at Emlyn, my son, and wonder whether he will ever make the grade as a footballer. I don't know, and I don't actually place too much importance on it. I'll be happy if he feels fulfilled in whatever job he takes on. But I do know that I would rather see Emlyn be a George Best for ten years than a workmanlike, grafting professional for twenty years. The pleasure that George gave during his short career far outstrips that provided by fifty lesser players who each played twice as long. I know that Shanks would have had the same attitude, and I think that is the key to how he would have handled Besty.

As with a marriage, it's people with different temperaments that sometimes get on best. George and Bill were quite opposite in many ways and could have worked together. Steve Davis was another who presented many opposite faces to those of Bill Shankly. North versus south, brash confidence versus modest uncertainty – but both brilliant when doing what they were best at.

Steve's manager, Barry Hearn, has becomes Steve's friend over the years. There's no doubt in my mind that Bill would have filled the same role for "the boy" as he would have called him. And in that friendship would have emerged the common knowledge that they both enjoyed their sport. Bill goes down in the history books as saying that football wasn't a matter of life and death – it was much more serious than that. But he also knew that sport was to be respected and enjoyed. Furthermore Bill would have recognised that he had a winner in Steve. I'm not saying he would have been over the top in his praise for the young Cockney, but he wouldn't have let his achievements go unnoticed by the world as has happened, to a certain degree, in Steve's own case.

"Good for each other" has to be the answer if Bill and Steve had ever got together. Both at the top, and both with minds ready to open up to new experiences.

I've been speaking about Bill as if he was the greatest manager ever. In my opinion he was. This, however, should not obscure the fact that, once in a while, I thought he talked a load of nonsense. Not often, not even occasionally, but once in a while. I can remember nudging John Toshak in a team meeting and raising my eyes to the ceiling in horror as Bill went into an explanation of some new master plan or other. We knew there was no point in arguing with him; the best we could do was to nod agreement and then totally forget what he'd said. If things came out all right on Saturday afternoon, who cared if it had been Bill's plan or a minor example of player-power? Bill would take the credit anyway!

The reason it was easy to cope with a man like Bill and his odd relapse was that you knew that he was being totally honest. Everything he said came from the bottom of his heart. He shone with sincerity. This was probably one reason he inspired such loyalty, and also his key to good relations with the press. It would also have been the greatest possible bonus to a player like Nora Perry. Someone to trust, someone consistently to give you an honest answer would have been great for Nora. It wouldn't have done Mike Gatting much harm either.

I've spoken to Mike when he's been up in the air with happiness, his confidence sky-high. I've also seen him down, battered by the trials of being England cricket captain. Bill would have had the good sense to have left Mike alone when things were going well, but would have been able to step in as the pressures from outside began to take their toll. When everything around you is seemingly falling apart you need somebody whom you can trust and somebody who speaks the same language as you. For me, and for Gatts, we would have first turned to our families. But having Bill inside the game made all the difference to me, and it would have done the same for Mike. You knew he was going to be honest and that he was not to be swayed by the winds of fashion. A great comfort and a great confidence-booster.

Perhaps we're edging here towards a mention of the press. Bill knew they had a job to do and helped them as best he could. He provided them with great quips and quotes and they gave him a platform for promoting his team. He understood why they printed nonsense from time to time and could live with that, but he wouldn't have liked gossip and scandal being attached to members of his club. The real test of his tolerance would have come if he had been team manager for Her Royal Highness The Princess Royal. The "pack" of royal watchers would have driven him to distraction. Bill had great respect for the Royal Family. "Great people" was his opinion. He especially warmed to The Princess Royal because of her sporting interests and her obvious ability.

I think Bill would have allowed the interviews and photo-sessions to take place, but he would have made quite sure that he stood in with "his" new player. Any silly questions would have been met with a stony glare. He'd also have made sure that his royal recruit was treated no differently from any other member of the team. This would not be for The Princess Royal's sake, because she wouldn't want any special attention anyway. It would be simply to convince the press and the world at large that he was dealing with a team game and not solely with individuals. A team is a collection of members, each as important as the next.

Bill's philosophy, which I've always tried to pass on to others, is that a team does not really depend on its stars. A team is as good as its poorest player. He's the one who holds the key and who can, with an error, lose a match for you.

Eventing is an interesting mix of individual and team sport. Bill, of course, was the expert at bringing the best out of a team. Would he have been so good, however, at dealing with those in intensely solo sports like darts or athletics?

Bill and John Lowe? I'm not sure. John's attitude to sport is unique amongst all the top achievers I've met. That he didn't take up darts until he'd left school and that he knows exactly when he is going to retire would have been strange to Bill. I think it all comes down to sporting ability. Ultimately Bill would have had great respect for John, understanding him or not, simply because of his great success at his chosen sport.

John is also happy to turn off from sport when he goes home. This was never Bill's way. When he eventually got home his long-suffering wife would be pressed into action to make a cup of tea. This would be so that Bill could sit and watch some videos of football matches. I have a feeling that John Lowe would turn off the darts if they came on television.

Another of the same persuasion is Nigel Mansell. On the race track he's giving everything he's got. Once off it, and out of overalls, it's golf, his family and his helicopter flying that take up his time. Racing is something he does for money and something he wants to become the best at. . .but it's not everything.

Another interesting aspect of Nigel is the unfortunate way he has just missed out on the World Drivers' Championships on more than one occasion. I know that Bill would have had something to say about this. In his book coming second could become a habit, and he didn't want his team getting bad habits. Bill could do nothing about burst tyres and freak accidents but the money in my pocket says that a Williams–Honda–Shankly team would have clinched that title.

Sandy Lyle shares with both John Lowe and Nigel Mansell the experience of playing in a loner sport. It's in these intensely personal contests, of games like golf and darts, that the players must be on top of their game, and on top of their emotions. Bill and Sandy would have got on well together, not least because Sandy is such a nice man. But, over and above that, I think Bill would have seen the strengths of the British golfer and would have created an atmosphere for him in which he could thrive. I like to think, but I'm not sure on this one, that Sandy would have peaked a bit earlier than he did under the guiding hand of The Boss. Who can tell?

In a similar way to Nigel Mansell, Sebastian Coe has had trouble in winning races that seem to be his for the taking. I can safely say that Bill and Seb would get on well, once Bill had knocked some sense into Seb about Chelsea. And I also know that Bill would respect Seb for the effort he puts into training.

Just how Shanks would manage to bring out the best in Seb, I'm not sure. But he'd be working with the best material available and would surely find the key to success very quickly. Most of all, I think Bill and Seb would just feel comfortable in each other's company. They could talk about great performances of the past, could gossip about mutual friends in the game and could enjoy sharing their ideas about the development of sports outside their own. Bill would be content. He'd have a great athlete in his team and a good companion too.

Bill always wanted the best of course, and if they happened to be the biggest too, he was doubly made up. The time he signed big Bill Yeats is memorable for The Boss inviting the press to come and walk round his new player. Great copy for the papers, and a great boost for the team. I fondly imagine what Bill would have made of Frank Bruno. Frank could make even Yeatsie look underfed. I have no great theories of how Bill would get the best out of Frank; I just chuckle at the thought of the discomfort he'd inflict on visiting teams by telling them just what Frank was going to do – and to whom – that afternoon. He'd turn Frank's presence in the team to a goal advantage every match.

Apart from one player, that is how I see Bill handling my "Great Britons". I've saved until last the one character that I think would have pleased Bill more than any other – Gareth Edwards. Gareth was the perfect player from Bill's point of view. He was individually brilliant but could play to a team plan. Bill often managed players who could fit in with his plans, and he sometimes had brilliant individualists on his books, but he rarely managed to find the right combination to satisfy his high standards. Kevin Keegan probably sums up the type of player best. His solo runs and quicksilver finishes bore the mark of genius but you never, for a moment, expected to see him resting on his laurels. Kevin would run and run after every ball and in support of every team-mate. Gareth, too, typifies that approach.

If Bill could choose just one of my "Great Britons" I suspect he would choose Gareth. Besty, possibly, but Gareth. . .almost certainly. He'd be delighted with his choice, too.

I can still remember the day that The Boss chose me to go to play for Liverpool. I didn't know it then but it was to prove the best move a footballer ever made. Playing for 'Pool and working under the best manager in the game, what more could I ask? Today I'm happy to acknowledge the great debt I owe Shanks. Without sentimentality, because that wasn't his style, but with great sadness, I just wish he was here today so we could have done a proper interview. "Son," he'd say, "write this down."

185

My Great Britons

World record holders, Olympic gold medallists, champion jockeys, Wimbledon winners. . .the people in this book are a bit special. Their sporting achievements are a part of what makes them "Great Britons", but it's not only in sport that these people excel.

Through doing the interviews I discovered that my "Great Britons" were special in any number of ways. Having spent a lifetime in professional sport, I wasn't too surprised to find this out. Sports people can be some of the kindest, most generous and funniest people I know. They also have some rather odd ways too. I hope that the book has shown up all of these points, and also indicated that sports stars, after all the hullabaloo, are only human. Of course they're all very dedicated to their sports, but they're also concerned with their families and friends, their homes and their hobbies. Some are also concerned with their waistlines and their fitness, but we won't say which amongst them.

Knowing the human side of the stars makes it easier for me to understand how upset they become, at times, with what is written and said about them. And it was this point that came out most strongly in so many of the interviews.

I don't want to go on about the press. After all, I'm part of the scene myself, writing a column for the *Daily Mirror*. There are two points that I want to make, however, and these were points that my "Great Britons" mentioned. The first is that the press don't spend enough time dealing with the sport itself, and the second is that the press are too quick to build somebody up, and then just as quick to knock them down again.

On the first point we must remember that Nigel Mansell, John Lowe, Nora Perry and all the other "Great Britons" are not just stars, they are *sports* stars. Without their achievements in sport they would not be newsworthy. So it should be the sport that receives the attention first.

Mike Gatting had more to complain about than most in the way the press treated the umpiring rows and other incidents on the ill-fated 1988 tour to Pakistan. He felt very upset when responsible papers were spending three-quarters of a report dealing with an incident with only a few lines devoted to the scores and performances on the field. Mike also saw the problem that journalists face with his ex-colleague, Mike Selvey. Selvey was covering the tour for a national daily paper and wrote some things that Gatts found hard to accept. When challenged, Mike Selvey pointed out the different perspective one suddenly has as a reporter rather than a player. The reporter is serving a different master.

It's no good me rattling on about what is wrong with sports coverage when I'm one of the people airing my views in the papers. In my column, however, I try to say things about the players and their sports performance; their private lives and personal habits are not my concern. If

I do want to criticise I hope I do it with humour and good intention. For example, half way through the 1987/88 season I remember suggesting that Terry Venables might need to change most of his current Tottenham Hotspur side if they were to become serious title challengers. Terry, through the *Sun* paper, got his own back at me. In the end, through headlines and articles, we had a good old ding-dong. But it was good-natured. I still admire and like Terry, and the issue was the ability of the Spurs side – nothing else.

So, if we are to have sensational headlines, let's keep to sports. Leave the rest aside. And let's also say something good about the stars. Nobody is suggesting that the "Great Britons" in this book are all angels. They're only human. However, it's not been hard to find good things to say about them. After all, they are all motivated by a love of sport and a desire to do well. There's nothing wrong in that.

Another thing I would not do in my column, and I don't like to see it elsewhere, is to overpraise a young sports star, only to bring him, or her, back down to earth a few months later. The sports business is hard enough without extra pressure coming from the press.

Will things get better? Well, I don't think they're *too* bad at the moment. But, as Seb Coe pointed out, we do sometimes get things out of perspective, and that's not always the fault of the press. He cited the example of Britain's Eddie Edwards. We all loved him for his heroic efforts and admired his courage at the 1988 Winter Olympics. Unfortunately his participation in the Games overshadowed some rather better performances than his. The sad fact, from Seb's point of view, was that the closing speech of the Games mentioned "The Eagle", and no other performer. An extreme case of wrong priorities, and not a good advertisement for sport.

And those are the last words I'm saying about sports coverage, the media and all that!

In fact it's almost the last grumble I'm going to allow anyone to have in this book. But there's one other point that I ought to make because all the people I interviewed raised it. This is the attitude of the young to sport.

Almost without exception, my "Great Britons" played sport, as a child, from morning till night. It was the same with me. All I ever wanted to do was kick a ball around. That may not be the best thing in the world to do, but it's got to be healthier and more fun than sitting watching television.

Somehow sport has lost out to the microchip. I never needed a video of a cup final because I was always involved in one in my back garden. And no computer fantasy game could be better than my own fantasies, of pulling on an England shirt and collecting an FA Cup winner's medal.

If I can put anything back into sport then I'd like it to be a contribution

189

to getting youngsters back into the parks, the sports halls and even the streets. I know I'm not alone in this. So many of the stars I spoke to agreed with me. If we produce a new star, a future "Great Briton", so much the better. But I'd be happy just to see more kids out there playing and enjoying sport.

And that's enough grumbling. Looking back at the interviews, I realised that there were some common characteristics. Some, like the hard work and energy that goes into becoming a "great", were not surprising. Others, however, did make me think. They say that you should never compete against a sports man or woman in anything, and that certainly seemed to be the case. My "Greats" were all bad losers in the sense that they didn't like losing – at anything. I felt sorry for some of their children who were destined to a life of defeat at games like snakes and ladders, ludo, cards and even beach cricket. I also felt sorry for anybody who tried to take my team of "Greats" on at football. Apart from myself, although I might decide to be the non-playing manager, we could field a side with Gareth Edwards (Swansea City), Mike Gatting (Watford), Sean Kerly, Seb Coe, John Francome and Frank Bruno, all of whom reckoned their chances as a professional before they moved to their specific sport. And there's also a young lad called George Best who, I'm told, is a bit useful.

Thinking of Besty, his was the one name that popped up at almost every interview. In most cases I never even had to mention him. Could it have been that I just happened to interview his fan club? The answer is, of course, that the little Irishman was a true born genius. They don't come along that often and so sports men and women who have been privileged to watch him tend to remember it. George has every right to feel pleased that so many other top sports stars admire him.

My admiration goes out to all of those whom I've included in the book. It's no secret, however, that I have one particular favourite in Her Royal Highness The Princess Royal. She's different class. I've always taken great delight in meeting her and I know that my family really enjoyed the weekend we spent at Gatcombe Park, her home and the venue for my interview. Apart from the pleasure of watching the horse trials and meeting the Princess, I recall the weekend for one other reason. For it was at Gatcombe that my son Emlyn became so overcome with nerves that he lost his appetite. Plates of sandwiches and slices of cake that normally would have disappeared in a moment were politely declined during tea with Her Royal Highness, family and friends. I should add that, by the time of a barbecue in the evening, matters had returned to normal and Barbara and I were having to explain to the chap doing the cooking that we did feed our children at home.

Her Royal Highness's involvement with charity work for numerous groups is well known. She would be the first to admit that her position in the country, and in the hearts of the British public, does help to bring attention to the plight of those for whom she is working. In a similar way, so many of my "Greats" have used their position in sport to do work for charity. The last thing they would want would be praise for their efforts. But let's make no mistake, British sports men and women, whether famous or not, have never been slow in supporting disadvantaged groups wherever they may be. My "Greats" are part of this tradition.

As mentioned above, young Emlyn, Emma and Barbara, my wife, came to Gatcombe. I'm an unashamed fan of family life, as, in fact, were several of the sports men and women I spoke to. In all my work I think of ways that I can involve my family, especially since I spend so much time away from home. In doing the book I recall a very special day I spent with Emma when we went to interview Nigel Mansell, who was accompanied by his family. And there was the time I took Emlyn to lunch with Mike Gatting. Emlyn is football mad, as opposed to his father who's a mad footballer, and soon realised that Mike shared his passion. Most of the time I was supposed to be interviewing was spent listening to Mike give young Emlyn tips about soccer. Mike obviously didn't trust Emlyn's father to help in this matter.

I can also remember well the day I nearly didn't interview Virginia Wade. I had fixed up to meet her at her home and turned up at the appointed time. Unfortunately she was out so I checked my arrangements and waited. As time passed I wondered what could be keeping her. I knew that both her time and mine was limited and started getting a little worried. As I paced up and down outside her front door I noticed a familiar looking woman open the door of the house next door and peer out anxiously. She glanced at her watch, looked around again, and went back inside. Then I recognised the face. . .it was Virginia Wade. I had got the wrong address! That was only slightly less awful than the first time I saw her. I was in my car when my passenger, John Toshak, shouted "Look, there's Virginia Wade." As I looked I took my eyes off the lorry parked in front of me with disastrous results. Ginny has suggested that we have a game of tennis next time I'm down her way. Does she know what she's letting herself in for?

Another amusing incident was when I was down in Clevedon to meet David Bryant. I'm not going to be unkind about Clevedon but it's hardly the Las Vegas of Avon. And the Pier Hotel certainly isn't Caesar's Palace. But this didn't matter because I was met with much kindness, especially by one man who said that it was so quiet in Clevedon that he thought it would be another hundred years before he had the chance to welcome another sports personality. I wished I had a camera to capture his face as David Bryant popped his head around the corner and said hello. It was a priceless moment.

David, as we all know, is apparently one of the calmest men around as he sucks on his unlit pipe and prepares to send down another match-winning wood. But David, like Seb Coe, will probably admit to being a bit like a swan on the water – gliding calmly across the surface but paddling like hell beneath. Not one of the sports stars said that it was easy.

They all worked and worked to reach the top. And then worked some more to stay there. My experience was the same. At the start of my career I couldn't trap a bag of cement, but I could run and run. And if effort alone was the yardstick, I'd say that I deserved the success I had.

If you're starting out on the road to the top there is no substitute for hard work. You've got to want success, you've got to be determined to achieve it and, when it really counts, you've got to be prepared to sacrifice everything to get it. Only then have you earned the right to achieve your ambitions – and earning the right to success is not the same as actually achieving it. The winners you've read about in this book will all testify, however, that it's all worth it. A life in sport is the best that there is.

And in talking about their lives I hope they have given something of the flavour of what it is that drives sports men and women on to the top, why they have been that extra bit special and why, in my book at least, they've become truly "Great" Britons.

Postscript

A few months will have elapsed between my writing these last few words, and you reading them. In that time we will have seen the best part of a cricket season, an FA Cup Final, the Seoul Olympics, the British Open. . .how the list could go on. Sport is like that. Nothing is forever, the record books will always be rewritten.

I feel, however, that my "Great Britons" are the kind of sports men and women who will not just be judged by their position in those same record books. My "Greats" will always represent that little something extra that makes sport such a valuable part of our way of life. It's to them that I want to address a few words of thanks.

Without hesitation or exception they accepted my invitations to talk. They entertained me in their homes, took me to their favourite restaurants and introduced me to their friends and families. They talked to me frankly and openly about their sports and their lives. In short, they were marvellous. To them all I extend my sincere thanks for helping me, and above all, helping sport in this country.

And also I'd like to thank all the other people involved in the writing of the book: my family, to whom the book is dedicated, for their patience; Graham Hart, for his help in the writing; and all at Partridge Press for their expertise in producing the finished article.

Thank you.